The Baptist Congregation

The Baptist Congregation

A Guide to Baptist Belief and Practice

Stanley J. Grenz

REGENT COLLEGE PUBLISHING
Vancouver

The Baptist Congregation
Copyright © Stanley J. Grenz

First published 1985 by Judson Press (ISBN 0-8170-1083-1)

This edition published 2002 by Regent College Publishing
5800 University Boulevard, Vancouver, B.C. V6T 2E4 Canada
www.regentpublishing.com

The views expressed in this work are those of the author and do not
necessarily represent the official position of Regent College.

Scripture is the author's own translation from the Hebrew and Greek
texts.

National Library of Canada Cataloguing in Publication Data

Grenz, Stanley, 1950-
  The Baptist congregation

  Includes bibliographical references.
  ISBN 1-55361-045-8 (Canada)
  ISBN 1-57383-060-7 (United States)

  1. Baptists—Government. 2. Sacraments—Baptists. 3. Baptists—
Doctrines. I. Title.

BX6340.G74 2002   286   C2002-910332-0

To the memory of my father,
The Reverend Richard A. Grenz,
faithful Baptist pastor for thirty-one years

Acknowledgments

As in the religious life, there is a corporate dimension to the production of any book. The author, therefore, wishes to acknowledge a debt of gratitude to the North American Baptist Conference leadership, who envisioned the project out of which this volume developed; to the North American Baptist Seminary community of students, administrators, and secretaries, who provided both important interaction with the manuscript and the necessary resources of time and personnel for its completion; and to my wife for patient support and encouragement.

Contents

Introduction

The Baptists are a people who share a common community life, marked in part by an understanding of the nature of the church which is uniquely theirs. This understanding flows from a basic conviction concerning the individual nature of the salvation experience and results in certain specific emphases concerning church ordinances and government. Fundamental commitments in these areas and their outworkings in the life of the community are termed "church polity."

This volume is offered as a statement of Baptist polity. It attempts to treat theological concerns seriously, while remaining nontechnical in approach. Although there is wide diversity among Baptists, the positions outlined herein reflect "mainline" Baptist thought, at least as far as that is possible. Likewise, the book is largely noncontroversial in tone, in that not every side of each issue discussed is presented and debated. Rather, the book seeks to build on the foundations of those emphases which have been significant throughout Baptist history, in order to provide a source book which may assist Baptist churches in their task of being a people of God in the closing decades of the twentieth century.

Baptists have always been concerned about issues of polity. In fact, the modern Baptist movement finds its source largely in the discussions of the English Puritans of the sixteenth and seventeenth centuries, which centered on polity questions. In the years since that time, many who have joined the Baptist ranks from other religious bodies have done so partly because they were confronted with issues of polity and found among this group convictions in these areas which they came to believe were consistent with New Testament principles.

Some Baptists suggest that polity is the only factor that separates them from other Protestant traditions. In the seventeenth century the English Calvinist Baptists utilized the Westminster Confession, which had been produced largely by their Presbyterian counterparts. Only the sections dealing with polity were altered when the document was adopted for use in Baptist congregations. Denominational differences, however, include more than external polity issues—the requisite age of baptismal candidates and the amount of water necessary—which are so often the focus of discussion. Nevertheless, it is in the area of polity that the uniqueness of the Baptist tradition is most readily visible.

Some relegate the Baptist insistence on their unique convictions in matters of polity to the status of an outmoded stubbornness, incompatible with an ecumenical age. In response it must be underscored that for all Christian faith groups church polity is significant, for it is an outgrowth of fundamental religious understandings. For example, the inability of sixteenth-century Lutherans and Calvinists to agree on the mode of the Lord's presence in the Communion elements might appear insignificant unless one is aware of the Christology lying behind the viewpoint of each side. So also for Baptists, their convictions concerning the nature of the church, the ordinances, and church government are rooted in certain basic theological convictions.

It is the contention of this book that Baptist responses to what they perceive as significant questions of polity are the result of an attempt to hear and be obedient to the voice of the Lord of the church as he speaks in the New Testament. As conscientious and sincere Christians, Baptists are concerned that God be glorified. They believe that glory is brought to God as Christ's church fulfills the mandate entrusted to it, a mandate which includes the command to the church that "all things be done decently and in order." Convictions of polity constitute a response to this command.

Further, Baptist polity arises out of a sincere attempt to follow consistently the implications of a fundamental understanding of the nature of God's claim on humanity. Baptists suggest that the call of the Creator is issued to individuals, is experienced individually, and demands an individual response. This understanding plays a significant role in determining Baptist convictions toward issues such as the nature of the church, the significance of the ordinances, and proper church government.

Differences of polity existing among the various Christian traditions are more than inconsequential arguments of nonessentials. This being the case, the way forward for all Christians cannot be that of blindly overlooking the heritage of each confessional group in the name of community and unity. Rather, true ecumenical progress within the wider body of Christ for the cause of Christ requires that each Christian be immersed in an understanding of one's own unique heritage and see that heritage in part as God's gift to the entire body. At the same time each Christian must be open to seek to understand each other Christian within that other person's confessional heritage, which also can become the voice of the Spirit speaking to the entire body of Christ.

It is, however, in the corporate life of the local congregation that convictions of polity will find their most obvious outworking. Most local churches carry a denominational label or enjoy denominational fellowship. Whenever this is the case, the responsibility falls on the congregation to become thoroughly knowledgeable of its own heritage within a confessional body for two reasons. On the one hand, denominational practice constitutes to some extent a standard for those local bodies who choose to utilize the denominational name. On the other hand, since all such standards are constantly developing and therefore can never be seen as finalized and fixed, the decisions, convictions, and actions of member congregations contribute to the further molding of the denomination. Each congregation must take seriously its role in this process knowing that this task requires both an openness to the voice of the Lord, who speaks through the Bible to the contemporary situation, and an awareness of the responses of denominational forebears to that same voice in the past.

Finally, polity is significant in the same way Christian theology is significant. Just as theological convictions shape life in the present, so also polity, which includes a community's theology of the church, its ordinances, and its government, significantly determines the response of the church in its own contemporary environment. Convictions concerning polity provide the structural framework in which and through which the people of God perceive their world and chart the possible courses of action that are available to them.

The church is confronted by an era of unparalleled opportunity and unparalleled peril. To meet this challenge, the people of God must continually remind themselves of their identity, their calling, and the divine resources available to them. In this endeavor the Baptists, with their unique heritage, have an important role. Therefore, an awareness on the part of Baptists of the special understanding of their tradition concerning the church, its ordinances, and its government is of utmost importance in these turbulent times.

I   The Essence of The Church

1 ❋ The Nature of the Church

"Church" is a word with which every believer is familiar. In spite of the familiarity of the term, however, for some it remains a confusing concept. Disagreement and misunderstanding surround many aspects of the church's existence in the world. Since the Reformation, Protestant groups have differed with one another and with other Christian faith groups on questions of church polity, such as the proper form of church government and the significance of the sacred observances. In recent years additional issues have surfaced, including spiritual gifts and ordination. More basic than these debates, however, are the divergent opinions concerning the very nature of the church itself. Commonplace in Western society is the erroneous equation of the term "church" with a building in which Christians meet or with an organization that Christians maintain. These understandings are quite different from that of the early believers. Foundational to the construction of any theology of the church is an understanding of what this term was originally intended to mean.

Although the word "church" is most generally associated with the New Testament, the concept itself actually originates in the Old Testament, in the self-consciousness of the people of Israel, who saw themselves as having a special relationship to God. One significant aspect of this relationship is expressed by the Hebrew word *qahal*. Although it is often used in the general sense of "assembly," this term occasionally carries a religious meaning, especially when it occurs in the form of "the congregation of Yahweh"

(Deuteronomy 23:1; 1 Chronicles 28:8). It is likely that this idea formed the background to Jesus' promise to build his church (Matthew 16:18), a promise which the New Testament authors saw as being fulfilled in their day in the fellowship of the disciples of the Lord.

As the circle of Jesus' disciples expanded into the Greek-speaking world, the early Christians found in that language a term which expressed well their understanding of their corporate identity. This term, *ekklēsia*, had been used to translate *qahal* in the Greek translation of the Old Testament scriptures (the Septuagint). As with its Hebrew counterpart, *ekklēsia* means "assembly." Originally it denoted the assembly of Greek citizens who were called out of their homes to the marketplace by a herald. This is reflected in the etymological roots of the term, for *ekklēsia* is derived from the verb "to call" (*kaleō*) and the preposition "out of" (*ek*), hence "those called out" or "those assembled." The early Christians saw themselves as "the people assembled, the called out ones" in a special sense, for they were the assembly of those called out by the proclamation of the gospel for the purpose of coming together to belong to God through Jesus the Christ. It is this term which is translated "church" in our English New Testament. Therefore this usage should form a basis of our understanding of our corporate identity as well. The church, then, is in the final analysis neither a building nor an organization, but people. The early Baptists, with this understanding in mind, referred to the buildings in which they met as meeting houses and not churches.

This basic meaning of the church is highlighted further by the various phrases and metaphors by which the New Testament writers describe this company. One such description is "the people of God" (1 Peter 2:9). The source of this phrase is the status of national Israel in the Old Testament era. Just as Israel was to be God's in a special way, so the disciples of Jesus were his. Christ's church is a group of people who are called to have a special status with a special task and responsibility. A second phrase, "temple of God" (Ephesians 2:19-22; 1 Peter 2:5), likewise is rooted in the Old Testament. The physical temple located in Jerusalem, like its predecessor, the tabernacle, was associated with the earthly presence of Yahweh (2 Chronicles 6:1-2). In the New Testament era, however, the focal point of God's presence could no longer be linked to a physical structure, for it was and still is now to be seen in the worldwide community called the church, the people who confess the name of Jesus.

A third phrase is one which is so commonly used that we tend to forget its metaphorical nature, namely, the phrase "the body of Christ" of which he is "head" (Colossians 1:18; Ephesians 5:23; 1 Corinthians 12:13ff.). In contrast to the other two, the background for this metaphor is not the Old

Testament, but rather human anatomy. The relationship between the body and the head illumines the relationship which should exist between Christ, the risen Lord, and the community of his disciples. The church, in other words, exists solely to do the will of Christ and to be the vehicle for the ongoing fulfillment of his purposes.

The meaning of the church is further seen in the usage of the term itself. First, some suggest that "church" may refer to an ideal company, "the mystical church," the one eternal fellowship of all believers, the total company of the redeemed (Hebrews 12:22-23). It is perhaps this ideal which Paul envisioned in his descriptions of the church in Romans 11:11-24 and in his epistles to the Ephesians and Colossians. Although somewhat controversial, this suggested usage is significant in that it underscores the fundamental unity of the people of God which transcends time. Second, "church" may refer to the universal church, the one fellowship of all believers on the earth. In this understanding the fundamental unity of the faithful across political, sociological, and spatial boundaries is underscored. Finally, "church" is used to indicate a specific local fellowship of believers who together constitute a congregation. The majority of occurrences of the word in the New Testament are in this category.

This threefold use of "church" is highly significant. It suggests that the essence of "church" should not be relegated to any one of the above to the exclusion of the others, nor should the importance of any of the three aspects be minimized. This implies that each local congregation is to be the church, just as the mystical church and the universal church are. All that is to be true of "church" in general is likewise to be true of each local congregation. The lofty Pauline statements about the body of Christ are intended to be made concrete in each local body. The local congregation, in other words, is to be the church of Jesus Christ in miniature.

In a similar way this threefold usage invests great significance in the various associational organizations, which are established by local congregations. As expressions of the wider fellowship of believers, these constitute to some extent manifestations of the church universal and therefore carry the great responsibility of reflecting, according to their individual purposes, the very nature of Christ's worldwide body.

A further significant starting point in the attempt to understand the meaning of the church is the concept of the kingdom of God. That this is the case is not surprising since Jesus' own message centered on announcing God's Kingdom. In contrast to our modern understanding of the word, which stresses the political domain or land mass over which a king rules, "kingdom" in both Old and New Testaments refers primarily to the inherent right of a king to exercise dominion. Secondarily it refers to the realm over which this kingship is extended. Hence, the kingdom of God is first of all God's exclusive right to exercise sovereignty over creation, a right which has been challenged and even denied by Adam's rebellious children. Secondly, God's kingdom is that area of creation in which God's will is being pursued.

Jesus came as the Suffering Servant of God, proclaiming God's rule and demanding that his hearers repent and open their lives to that rulership, which would one day be universally acknowledged. The obedient response to this demand brings the church into existence, as persons are joined together by their common allegiance to Jesus as Lord and by their desire to bring about obedience to the will of God in their own lives and in the world as a whole. Because of their obedience such persons constitute a special domain over which God is acknowledged as sovereign in a special sense. They are to be a sign in this fallen world of the new age which God will bring to pass when Jesus returns.

This commitment to God and to the doing of God's will entails a self-understanding which emphasizes pilgrimage. The church is always "en route," never attaining the perfect state of existence which it awaits, and therefore always eager for reformation and renewal. It does not look back to some ideal in the past but always looks forward to the goal which awaits it in the new creation. It is never satisfied with victories won and tasks completed but always moves on to new skirmishes with the powers of darkness and new responsibilities under the authority of the Lord. The church always keeps in view the vision of the new creation when God's rule will be complete and universal. With this vision before it the church seeks to mirror in the present the coming kingdom of God, the glorious divine rule of righteousness, justice, and love.

In addition to the meaning of the word *ekklēsia*, the metaphors used to describe this company, the three usages of the term and the concept of God's kingdom, the nature of the church also arises out of the nature of God. Christian theology emphasizes that the eternal God is not solitary singleness. Rather, the Divine One revealed to us is "trinity" and therefore "community." The message of the Bible constitutes an invitation to us to share in this life-in-community, and out of this invitation arises the community called the church. In his prayer for the disciples Jesus expressed this truth, for his concern was that the community and unity which he shared with the one he called "Father" be experienced among his followers (John 17:21). Further, the divine community is characterized by love, for this is the relationship shared by the three persons of the Godhead. For this reason the church is also to be characterized by mutual love among its members (e.g. Philippians 2:1-4). In short, the church, which is called into being by God, is called to be a mirror to the world of God's own nature.

2 The Purpose of the Church

It has been suggested that the church of Jesus Christ is the assembly of those who have been called out by the proclamation of the gospel to belong to God; it is the company of those who have placed themselves under the rulership of God and who desire to have God's will, God's kingship, actualized in their lives and in the world as a whole. With this understanding of the nature of the church in mind, the overarching purpose of the body of Christ can be more fully outlined.

The Mandate Given to the Church

Foundational to an understanding of the purpose of the church is the question concerning the purposes of God in creation and in history. The biblical authors are clear in affirming that the entire created order is designed with the glory of God in view. God's handiwork stands as a witness to God's glory and has as its purpose the glorification of the Creator (e.g., Psalm 19:1-4). God's activity in history has the same goal in view. Yahweh's dealings with humanity under the old covenant were climaxed by the coming of Jesus, whose life was dedicated to the task of advancing the divine will. This viewpoint runs through the entire New Testament. In fact, John's Gospel speaks of Jesus' mission specifically in terms of the glorification of the one he called "Father" (John 17:1-5).

The coming of Christ resulted in the gathering of a people who had experienced reconciliation with God. Paul placed God's action for saving lost sinners within the context of God's glory, for we are redeemed in order to glorify God and to be a showcase of the grace of the one who saved us in Christ (Ephesians 1:5-6, 11-14; 2:6-7). If the purpose of creation as a whole and the purpose of God's saving activity in history are related to God's glory, then it would follow that the fundamental purpose of the church is the same, namely, to bring glory to God (Ephesians 3:10-11, 21). It is for this glory that the church is called into existence and continues to exist in the world. Therefore, the ultimate motivation, purpose, and design of every church activity and undertaking ought to be that of seeking to glorify our Maker and Savior. Since each local congregation is the church of Jesus Christ in miniature, the goal of each activity of each local body ought to be the desire to bring glory to God.

At this point the question arises as to how this is accomplished in the church. Here again a proper understanding of God's kingdom is of assistance. God desires a people who are concerned about the fulfillment of the will of the Creator. Glory is brought to the Sovereign of the universe as God's will is carried out. Thus, the church fulfills its purpose of glorifying God as it is diligent in doing the divine will, that is, as it is active in completing the mandate specifically entrusted to it in the program of God. From the New Testament one can conclude that this mandate is threefold.

First, the people of God have been entrusted with a mandate of worship (John 4:23-24). Basically, the term "worship," arising from the idea of "worth-ship," means attributing worth to one who is worthy. That worship has become a lost art in contemporary Western society is woefully evident. However, true worship of God is gloriously illumined in various texts in the Bible (e.g., Isaiah 6 and Revelation 4,5), many of which give insight into the nature of the One to whom worship is due. For example, worth is often attributed to the Holy One, the One who is transcendent over all of creation, morally pure and upright in dealing with all creatures (e.g., Revelation 4:6-8). Further, worth is attributed to the One who created all things and therefore is worthy of receiving praise from all creatures (4:9-11). Homage is likewise to be paid to Jesus, the Savior, because he has purchased our salvation (5:6-12).

Worship is to play an important role in the life of the church, both as an individual act and as a corporate activity. The church gathered is to be a place where true worship transpires. Corporate worship can assume various forms, such as music, declaration, and prayer. Music is a suitable form of worship (e.g., Psalm 149:1-3) when the lyrics and music are offered as praise and thanksgiving to the transcendent and active God who has done glorious things. Worship occurs in the form of declaration when the Christian community seeks to give verbal expression concerning God's grace and goodness (1 Peter 2:9). Corporate prayer is an act of worship when its content centers on God's majesty and faithfulness, thereby becoming an expression of praise, thanksgiving, and petition. Of course, the worship value of any of these activities is lost when God is displaced as the focal point or when other motives replace the desire to attribute worth to God.

The second sphere of the church's mandate is edification. While worship is intentionally God-directed, edification is directed to the congregation itself ("inward-directed"). Edification consists of the members of the body of Christ ministering to one another so that all might develop spiritually. Jesus modeled true edification in his own ministry to his disciples, a ministry which climaxed in his willingness to wash their feet and then die for their salvation. Paul articulated the goal of the entire edification enterprise as being that of bringing each member of Christ's body to full maturity (Ephesians 4:11-13).

Basically there are two ways in which the edification mandate is accomplished. First, edification entails concern for the physical and material needs of others. This is repeatedly stressed in the New Testament. So important is this task that involvement in it is a measure of the presence of God's love (1 John 3:17); it is ranked in importance with verbal praise to God (Hebrews 13:15-16); and it will be a basis of final judgment (Matthew 25:40). Second, the edification mandate includes concern for spiritual and psychological needs. The ministries of burden lifting (Galatians 6:1-2), intercessory prayer (James 5:16), and encouragement and admonition (Hebrews 10:24-25) are to be practiced. Edification is one of the goals of the church's preaching and teaching ministries. This same end is also served by a variety of other activities, such as visitation, small group experiences, and even the genuine interest of the membership in the lives of others (e.g., Philippians 2:4).

The third mandate is directed outward toward other people. This task, that of outreach, encompasses two interrelated and inseparable aspects. On the one hand, outreach takes the form of disciplemaking, a mission to which the risen Lord called his people (Matthew 28:19-20). Proclaiming the gospel message, bringing others into the fellowship, and teaching new disciples the ways of the Lord are all necessary elements in this evangelistic enterprise. On the other hand, outreach entails ministry to the world. Just as Jesus saw himself and his work in terms of servanthood to others (see Luke 4:16-21), so also his body, the church is called to serve humanity in his name. In this task the disciple can claim the promise of the Lord himself that his followers would do even greater works than he did, because of the presence of the Spirit in the community of faith (John 14:11-12).

Identifying Characteristics of the Church

A discussion of the meaning and purpose of the church naturally includes the question of the identifying characteristics, or the "marks" of the true church, an issue which, in spite of its antiquity (dating back to the writing of 1 John 2:18) is still debated today. Traditionally three major opinions have received wide adherence. The first suggests that the true church is marked by apostolic succession. In this view a local congregation belongs to the true church as it stands in fellowship with a church official (specifically a bishop), whose ordination is determined by "apostolic succession" through the early apostles to Christ himself. The Protestant Reformation was in part a reaction against this "high" ecclesiology as developed by the medieval church. Many Reformation churches adopted a second position, in which the true church is marked by word and sacrament; the church is present where the Word of God is properly proclaimed and the sacraments are properly administered. A third model, adhered to by most Baptists, declares that the church is marked by believers standing in covenant with God and one another.

This third understanding follows most naturally from what has been said thus far. If the *ekklēsia* is the assembly of people called out by the proclamation of the gospel to belong to God through Jesus the Christ, and if belonging to God entails the threefold mandate of actualizing God's will in worship, edification, and outreach, then the church of Jesus Christ is present wherever believers have united together for the purpose of carrying out their corporate mandate. The church, then, is a covenant community, a group of believers who have covenanted with God to live as a community under God's rulership and to strive as a body to be obedient to God's will.

In prior generations Baptists were keenly aware of this covenant relationship and gave expression to it through periodic "owning" of the covenant by the entire congregation. Baptists today would do well to recapture this spirit of the corporate standing of God's people before their Creator and Savior and of their responsibility to one another as members of the one community.

The concept of the church as consisting of people is emphasized in the writings of the New Testament. In employing the metaphor from the temple of God, Peter suggested that the church is being constructed from individual "living stones" (1 Peter 2:5). Paul declared that the church as Christ's body consists of its individual members, each of whom is important to the whole (1 Corinthians 12:12ff.).

Paralleling this emphasis, however, is an equally significant stress on the importance of church leaders as constituting a foundational core of the people of God. The Gospels and the book of Acts indicate that a certain primacy was given to Peter and the twelve in the infant church. This fact is vividly seen in Jesus' response to Peter's confession of His messiahship (Matthew 16:15-19). In spite of attempts to find some other significance in this text, Jesus' words are best understood as a prophecy of Peter's key role in the future development of Christ's community, a role which is clearly portrayed in the opening chapters of Acts. Of course, there is neither textual nor theological warrant for the suggestion that Peter's position is to be passed on to future persons, as the Roman Catholic Church maintains.

The foundational role of church leaders is also outlined in the Pauline literature, which underscores the importance of apostles and prophets (Ephesians 2:19-20), of an ordering of gifted people in the body (1 Corinthians 12:28; Ephesians 4:11), and of local congregational leaders (see, for example, the Pastoral Epistles). At the same time, the New Testament is clear in asserting that the leadership role is not to be a source of pride nor to be used for personal gain. Rather, Jesus remains the model of leadership, and his example is one of servanthood for the sake of others.

The New Testament concept of the church balances the emphasis on the people as a whole with an emphasis on leaders serving the whole. This concept entails a further balance between a stress on the individual and the principle of interdependency. As was stated above, both Peter and Paul in keeping with Jesus' own individual-centered ministry and proclamation spoke of Christ's body as composed of individuals. Similarly, the term "church" in the New Testament is generally used to refer to a local congregation, thereby emphasizing the singular, local church. Nevertheless, this biblical stress must not be interpreted in terms of the modern individualistic outlook—whether in regard to the individual believer or the individual church—since in the New Testament individualism is placed within the context of interdependency. Throughout Scripture the believer is not viewed as an isolated person, but rather as a participant in the whole. Peter spoke of "living stones" as being fitted together into the one structure, and Paul viewed individual members in terms of their presence in the whole body. The stress in both cases is on individual participation in the corporate life.

In the same way, the local congregation is not to be viewed in isolation from other congregations, but rather as a local manifestation of that corporate entity which is also manifested in other localities and in the joint life of the wider fellowship. All congregations are a part of all others, just as all believers are interdependent. This theme surfaces in Paul's epistles in various ways. For example, the Gentile churches are to contribute to the support of the Jerusalem church (Romans 15:26-27), and the Corinthian congregation is to take note of what is commonly practiced by all the churches of Christ (1 Corinthians 11:16).

In short, the true church is marked by people, the assembly of those who have been called out by the proclamation of the gospel to belong to God through Jesus. As such, they are to be a people with a special consciousness of covenant and community. Conscious of their standing under the lordship of Christ as those who confess that "Jesus is Lord to the glory of God the Father," they share a common commitment to one Lord, to one threefold purpose, and to one another. In this body, recognition is given to the foundational status of the early leaders (apostles and prophets) and to the importance of the guidance of contemporary leaders as appointed by Christ. A healthy community consciousness binds all Christians together, disallowing in the body of Christ the "hyper-individualism" so prevalent in our culture. No individual Christian dare deny the need for the church community, and no individual church dare suggest it needs no affiliation with other congregations. The church of Jesus Christ is one mutually interdependent body, the community of faith.

The Formation of a Congregation

Since the church is the assembly of those called out by the gospel to belong to God in Christ, the privilege of forming a local expression of Christ's body resides in the company of believers, apart from any external hierarchy. Hence, should God call forth such a group in any given location to covenant together as a community of faith for the purpose of carrying out the mandate of the people of God, a church can be formed.

The actual formation of a congregation has been seen among Baptists as involving three stages. First, a body of believers begins to meet together for study, prayer, and worship, and through this process senses the desire to enter into formal covenant with one another and God. Next, the group formulates its desire in a document called a constitution, which will guide the group in orderly government. This document should include the following features:

A. Constitution proper
  1. Official, legal church name
  2. Purposes of the church
  3. Denominational affiliation (intended, at this stage)
  4. Membership procedures: means for congregational acceptance and dismissal of members, privileges and responsibilities of members, discipline of members
  5. Decision procedures
     a. leadership decisions—congregational selection and dismissal of leaders (including pastoral staff), including provision for nominating and pulpit committees
     b. financial decisions—congregational approval of budget and expenditures, including purchase and sale of legal property

6. Amendment procedure

B. Appendixes: church covenant and statement of faith

C. Bylaws (additional procedural matters)

1. Listing of church boards, additional committees, and officers, with responsibilities and selection and termination procedures
2. Listing of regular church meetings: worship, study services; business meetings, including quorum and system of rules of order
3. Financial resources program, including establishment of fiscal year (calendar year, if possible)
4. Listing of auxiliary organizations, including purposes, officers, and relation to the church
5. Provision for amendments

Third, the body of believers submits the proposed constitution to the regional association for structural and legal advice. At this point formal membership procedures can be initiated (e.g., transfer letters from other congregations are solicited and arrangements are made for the baptism of new believers). After these steps have been completed, all who desire to unite together in the new congregation meet to adopt the constitution, select officers, and seek associational recognition. This process climaxes in a recognition service.

At each stage of the founding of a new congregation, the balance between the autonomy of this local body and the interdependency principle ought to be maintained. Often the initial impetus for the coming together of such a group lies with another church or an association which sees the potential for a new congregation in a specific area. In such cases, interdependency receives expression almost as a matter of course as the advisory body and the potential congregation assist each other at each step. For example, the sponsoring association or parent church provides needed financial and personnel resources, expertise in church life, and a broader, outside perspective. In addition, the local group supplies a keen awareness of community needs and potential as well as a vision for the future of the proposed congregation. When a local group arises in a more spontaneous fashion, contact with and sponsorship by some outside church or association ought to be established as early as feasible, so that additional resources and advice become available and expression is given to the unity of the local body with the wider fellowship.

At the second and third stages, the association continues to provide significant services to the local group. Because it is aware both of denominational practice and of civil laws, the regional body is in a position to offer valuable assistance in the formation of congregational structures and legal documents which will be of lasting usefulness. Similarly, association advice and support can facilitate the local body as it organizes itself, holds elections, and establishes a membership roll. In all of this, however, the supportive function of the larger body must not be overlooked. It must always be kept in mind that it is the local group that is acting under the advice of the association.

II ❋ The Ordinances of the Church

3 ❀
The Nature of
the Ordinances

Baptists, following Reformed tradition, practice two sacred observances—baptism and the Lord's Supper. Most refer to these acts as "ordinances" rather than as "sacraments," which is the more broadly used term. However, there is a growing movement among some Baptists to reemploy the word rejected by our denominational forebears, reopening the question concerning the nature of these acts and their proper description.

The Significance of the Ordinances

"Sacrament" is derived from the Latin, *sacramentum*, which originally referred to a soldier's oath to his commanding officer to be faithful and obedient until death. This word came to be seen by the church as aptly expressing the nature of the church's sacred rites. A sacrament was an outward and visible sign of an inward and spiritual grace.

The religious use of the term developed as the church sought to determine exactly how baptism and the Lord's Supper were used by God in the believer's life. By the Middle Ages common belief held that the sacraments themselves were able to infuse the grace of God into the participant regardless of the spiritual condition (the faith) of either the recipient or the administering clergy. In the Reformation this prevailing opinion was called into question when Luther declared that faith was necessary for the effective operation of any sacrament. Subsequent reaction to the "magical" understanding of the Middle Ages went ever further, climaxing in the total rejection of any suggestion that the acts themselves produced some effect. Baptism and the Lord's Supper came to be seen solely as symbols of a deeper spiritual reality that comes about wholly independent of the rites themselves. With this change in understanding came a change in terminology as well; "sacraments" became "ordinances."

The term "ordinance" is indeed a meaningful term. It is derived from "ordain" and thus refers to those acts which Christ himself instituted for his disciples to practice. In this way some resemblance to the original secular concept of *sacramentum* is maintained, since baptism and the Lord's Supper are signs of the disciple's willing obedience to the Lord's command.

Despite the appropriateness of the word "ordinance," the relegation of baptism and the Lord's Supper to the status of "mere symbols," as is sometimes the case among Baptists, has certain problems. First, this outlook is foreign to the thought of the New Testament. In the ancient world a symbol carried power, in that a sign was closely related to that which it signified. It pointed to the underlying reality and also was a means of communicating ideas and evoking a response. This is aptly illustrated by the caution which surrounded the use of personal names. The ancients were not given to divulging freely their own names to others, for it was thought that knowing the name of another entailed the ability to exercise a certain degree of power over that person. This understanding came to be applied to the ordinances of the church. As symbols, the sacred rites were seen as deeply significant means of participation in the reality symbolized. To be baptized in Jesus' name meant to be incorporated into the sphere of his being. Even his death could be shared by the believer by means of baptism (Romans 6:1-4). Obviously, then, any reduction of these divinely instituted practices to the status of "mere symbols" empties them of the profound meaning that they carried for Christians in the first centuries.

Second, the reduction of the ordinances to the status of being "mere symbols" results in a reduction of the value and importance placed on them. If a sacred practice is unrelated to the experiencing of the reality it symbolizes, one may rightfully question the need for faithful participation in it. This consideration has led certain groups to abandon the practice of the ordinances altogether and has resulted in a casual attitude toward participation in these acts among many who still observe them. It is sadly ironic that Baptists, whose name is derived from baptism, often see this act as an appendage to conversion, required merely for local church membership, and see presence at the Lord's Table as a matter of indifference. But if these acts are presented as having little significance except as "steps of obedience," neither the believing community nor society can be expected to place much value on them.

A balanced understanding of baptism and the Lord's Supper seeks to retain the concept of ordinance while recapturing the original meaning of sacrament. The rites employed in the church of Christ must find their basis in the fact that Jesus himself ordained them and their continued practice throughout the church age. In other words, only those practices which are ordinances of our Lord ought to receive this significant status.

The Lord did not leave these practices to his church without reason, however. Participation in the ordinances carries a deep significance, which may be seen as "sacramental" in various ways. First, these acts are significant as they become oaths of fidelity and obedience to our Commander even to the point of death. Baptism and subsequent participation in the Lord's Supper afford occasion first to affirm (baptism) and then repeatedly to reaffirm (Lord's Supper) personal loyalty to Christ. Second, the ordinances are of sacramental significance because the presence of the participant's faith allows them to become one means utilized by the Holy Spirit in the sanctification process. They can become channels for the Spirit's sovereign work in the mind, will, and heart of the believer. Third, the ordinances are sacramental as visual sermons. These acts are closely connected to the essential gospel message concerning the death and resurrection of Jesus and the need for new birth. This message is presented in the ordinances in the form of an object lesson, proclaiming the Word of God through picture and symbol.

Fourth, participation in the ordinances carries sacramental significance because of the symbolic relationship between these observances and God's saving actions. This relationship can be more readily grasped when understood in the context of Old Testament practices, such as the Passover. The Passover celebration, which was to be observed by all generations of Israelites, carried a symbolic relationship to God's action in the Exodus. By means of this rite, subsequent generations could symbolically participate in that saving event as members of the Covenant community. At the same time participants both anticipated divine actions on behalf of the community and were vividly reminded of the promise of God's continuing presence.

In an analogous way, Christian ordinances are symbolic reenactments of God's liberating action in Christ. Participation in the ordinances is a means to symbolic participation in this divine act. Yet, the focus of these observances is not only past, but also future. For this reason the ordinances are also "pre-enactments" anticipating God's future salvation, which will occur when history is brought to its triumphant goal in God's kingdom. Therefore, through the ordinances the believer participates symbolically in God's past and anticipates God's future even now in the present. In this way strength, hope, and courage to see God near and active in the present are available to the eyes of faith.

In summary, neither the sacramentarian outlook of the medieval church, which denies the need for personal faith in the working of sacred rites, nor any rationalistic reductionism, which sees no significance in participation in these acts, provides the best understanding. Rather, these acts are ordinances, practices continued because of the Lord's command and in obedience to him. They are also sacraments (in the original sense of the term), acts which carry profound gospel significance and are given to the church for the benefit of the people of God.

The Number of Ordinances

The Roman Catholic Church practices seven sacraments—baptism, confirmation, the Eucharist (Lord's Supper), penance, ordination, marriage, and the anointing of the sick. The Reformation churches reduced this number to two, baptism and Lord's Supper, although some Lutherans see penance as sacramental. Certain Mennonites practice footwashing as a sacrament, albeit one of less importance than the other two.

The understanding of these acts outlined above suggests the following criteria for determining which practices actually qualify as bona fide ordinances/sacraments. First, since any such practice is an ordinance, there must be scriptural evidence that Jesus instituted the rite and intended its continued observance in the church. Second, since the early Christians were the first to perpetuate any act which Jesus instituted, there must be evidence that the early church continued the practice commanded by the Lord. Finally, since a sacrament is significant only as it symbolizes the underlying reality, the rite must be so closely bound to the gospel message itself that it can become a visual sermon.

By these criteria both baptism and the Lord's Supper are without question ordinances of the church. Both were instituted by our Lord (see Matthew 28:19-20; Luke 22:19-20), practiced by the apostolic church, and aptly portray the gospel message. Footwashing may meet the first criterion, but there is no record of subsequent practice in the early church, and its link to the gospel message is weak. Baptists find no support for any of the other suggested sacraments. There is no indication that our Lord instituted the perpetual practice of any of them as sacred observances on the same level with baptism and the Lord's Supper; there is no evidence that the early church viewed any of these acts as ordinances; and the value of these acts as symbols of the gospel message is weak.

4 Baptism—The Initiatory Ordinance

Baptism has been practiced almost universally by the church of Christ since its inception in the first century and has generally been seen as being somehow linked with the initiation of an individual into the body of Christ. In spite of this basic unanimity, this ordinance has produced much disagreement among Christians. Some traditions understand baptism as a powerful means of grace, which the Holy Spirit utilizes in the process of regeneration. Others value the act as a sign and seal of God's promise of grace toward the participant. When used in the context of infant baptism, both of these interpretations risk the danger of two opposite errors—equating the act of baptism with regeneration or reducing baptism to infant dedication

While not necessarily denying the validity of the other two, Baptists emphasize a third understanding. Based on the intertwining of personal faith and baptism as its outward sign which they find in the New Testament, Baptists view this act as a public confession of personal faith on the part of the baptismal candidate. For them, baptism is the public response to the gospel and a sacred public testimony.

The Meaning of Baptism

In the Baptist understanding baptism comprises both a declaration of the gospel and a testimony of a personal, experiential reality. This understanding extends to three interdependent emphases present in the New Testament.

First, baptism as declaration and testimony signifies entry into the church of Christ (1 Corinthians 12:13). The church is unique in that it is comprised of those persons whose allegiance belongs to Jesus the Christ. Baptism is the divinely instituted public entry point into this confessing company. As a gospel declaration this act proclaims one significant aspect of the new birth, namely that the old allegiances are broken in order that a new, all-pervasive allegiance may be formed. As a personal testimony, baptism is the baptismal candidate's witness to the personal experience of this new birth. By this public act this person joins with the Christian community in declaring "Jesus is Lord" and expresses the desire henceforth to be numbered with that confessing community.

This aspect of baptism may perhaps be understood more readily when placed in the context of societies in which Christians suffer overt persecution. In such situations a person first experiences the brunt of opposition following the public act of baptism. In baptism a public statement is given concerning personal forsaking of the past for a new loyalty and a new community. For this reason baptism normally should include membership in the baptizing congregation.

Second, baptism signifies union with Christ in death and resurrection (Romans 6:3-4). As a gospel declaration, baptism proclaims that Jesus died and was resurrected to new life, and through union with him the believer dies to the old life and becomes alive to the new. As a public testimony this act is the candidate's witness to the reality of personal union with Christ.

Union with Christ in baptism is related to two other New Testament themes, forgiveness of sins and reception of the Spirit. Forgiveness is linked to baptism's status as a symbol of union with Christ's death (e.g., Acts 2:38) since this union brings separation from one's past and its sins and since Christ's death is God's covering for sins. The imagery of outward washing is an appropriate symbol for this theological truth. Similarly, the reception of the Holy Spirit and baptism as symbolic of the union of the believer with Christ in resurrection belong together. The Spirit is the new life in which the Christian participates, as one who is raised with Christ.

Third, baptism signifies the sealing of a covenant with God (1 Peter 3:21). This understanding formed a basis for the early Baptist emphasis on the church as a covenant community and baptism as the act by which the covenant is sealed. The ordinance speaks of renouncing Satan in order that a covenant might be made with a new Lord. It is likewise a public testimony to the reality of this new covenant in the life of the candidate, who in this act is publicly sealing a lifelong commitment to God.

The Impact of Baptism

Because baptism carries these three significant meanings, it can become dynamic in the hand of the Holy Spirit. As such it may produce an impact in three directions. First, for the baptismal candidate baptism can be an event to remember. Throughout one's subsequent life one can look back to the day of baptism and call to mind the serious commitment made. To assist in this, the baptizing community ought to make each observance of this rite a festive celebration filled with meaning.

Second, baptism can have an impact on the baptizing community. As a visual gospel proclamation the ordinance is a reminder of the grace which each believer has experienced. Each observance ought, therefore, to be a joyous occasion filled with thanksgiving and worship. Further, as a reminder of one's own baptismal pledge, each observance is an encouragement to each believer present to be faithful to that personal baptismal vow of loyalty. Likewise, as one who is now through baptism beginning the Christian pilgrimage, the candidate serves as a reminder to the community of the mandate it has received to edify this new believer and all believers until all attain the full stature of Christ (Ephesians 4:13). At the same time the baptismal candidate symbolizes the many in the world who ought to respond to the call of Christ, reminding the community of its unfulfilled outreach mandate.

Third, the general public can also experience the impact of the ordinance. Baptism, when practiced in conjunction with the verbalization of the gospel symbolized in the act, can become the voice of the Holy Spirit. As the baptismal candidate symbolically reenacts the facts of Jesus' death, burial, and resurrection, an implicit call is issued to the observer to make the same confession of faith in Jesus Christ now publicly being made by the one standing in the baptismal water.

The Subjects of Baptism

The manifold meaning of baptism ought to be a significant factor in determining the proper subjects of baptism. A preliminary question, however, is whether or not baptism is a prerequisite for participation in the coming kingdom of God. The Bible clearly indicates that many will be present in the redeemed society who have never been baptized in the Christian sense. The saints of the Old Testament and certain pre-Pentecost disciples of Jesus, such as the thief on the cross, stand as examples. The same may be the case for those who never develop to the point of making moral choices, such as those dying in infancy and the severely mentally retarded (see Deuteronomy 1:39; Numbers 14:29-31; Isaiah 7:15-16; Matthew 18:1-14; 19:14). Further, the New Testament is clear that not all who are baptized will be present among the company of the redeemed, since baptism alone constitutes no guarantee of kingdom participation (Acts 8:13, 23; Hebrews 6:4-6).

Nevertheless, the general thrust of the entire New Testament is that faith expressed in the outward act of baptism is so closely linked with the new birth as to be a significant aspect of the normal mode of entry into the kingdom of God. Baptism is the divinely given vehicle for public confession of personal commitment, for it is the outward testimony to the presence of inward faith (e.g., John 3:5; Acts 2:38).

Consistent with this linking of outward act with inward reality, the apostolic church apparently refused to separate baptism from personal conversion either logically or temporally. The question of the necessity of baptism for conversion was not even posed in the first century. Rather, the one who desired to become part of the people of God and to acknowledge Jesus as Lord quite automatically sought to express this by means of baptism. This act was normally completed as soon as feasible (Acts 2:38, 41; 8:35-38; 10:47; 16:33). In the mind of the early church, then, faith was not merely private decision, but personal commitment requiring public expression. This public aspect of faith was seen as an integral part of the conversion experience itself to the extent that until faith was confessed in baptism, conversion remained incomplete (hence, Mark 16:16; 1 Peter 3:21; Galatians 3:26-27). An "unbaptized Christian" was totally foreign to the understanding of the early church.

The relationship of private, inward commitment to its public expression can be illumined by an analogy to marriage. The marriage relationship is ultimately constituted by the inward commitment of two people to each other. Yet, integral to marriage is the public expression of this commitment. So also with conversion. Inward commitment to Jesus as Lord is sealed by the corresponding public expression before witnesses. Baptism in water is the practice given to the church by which this essential public witness is to be made. Although the doors of the kingdom are wide enough to accommodate those who for various reasons do not follow this pattern, faith expressed in baptism is the norm.

Most major Christian traditions suggest that it is proper to extend this outward sign both to adult converts and infants. Baptists, however, have adamantly denied the propriety of administering baptism to all but conscious believers. This position is built on various considerations, including biblical precedent and the dangers inherent in infant baptism. But the most significant basis for believer's baptism is the meaning of the ordinance itself.

In baptism the candidate is not only depicting in symbolic form the essence of Christian faith, but also is boldly giving personal public declaration to the presence of the underlying spiritual reality in that person's own life (entry into the church, union with Christ, sealing of a new covenant). Therefore, the conscious faith of the candidate is necessary, since without it the meaning ascribed to the rite cannot be present. For this reason the ordinance should be reserved for the one who can participate in this reality and make these public declarations.

The Mode of Baptism

Among Christian churches three modes of baptism are in use: pouring, practiced by certain Anabaptist bodies; sprinkling, practiced by the great majority of Western Christians; and immersion, practiced by many in the believer's baptism tradition as well as by the Orthodox Church (which immerses babies).

There is strong indication that immersion was employed by the New Testament church. The terms "baptize" and "baptism" are transliterations from the Greek term *baptizō*, meaning "to dip," "to immerse," or "to surround with," in contrast to *hrantizō*, "to sprinkle." Likewise, the description of baptisms found in the New Testament make reference to "going down into the water" and "coming up out of the water" (e.g., Acts 8:39 and Matthew 3:16; see also John 3:23). These New Testament considerations are significant and weighty, but they do not constitute a completely conclusive proof that immersion was the sole mode used in the first century, since "to baptize" is sometimes used in a figurative sense (e.g., Mark 7:4; 10:38-39; Luke 11:38; 1 Corinthians 10:2), and the descriptions fail to detail for us what actually transpired in the water. Immersion, however, has been the dominant commitment of the Baptist tradition although Baptists have not been unanimous in holding to it as the sole mode of valid baptism. The first modern Baptists, for example, the congregation of John Smythe, did not practice immersion for thirty years.

Additional insight concerning this issue, however, can be derived from the theological significance of the mode employed. Since baptism is a symbol and symbols are powerful as carriers of meaning, it follows that the symbol utilized should picture the reality symbolized as closely as is possible and practical. This being the case, immersion looms as the best of the three modes currently practiced. More vividly than either pouring or sprinkling, immersion depicts the burial and resurrection of Jesus, the severing of ties with the old life in order to seal a covenant with God, and the public confession of personal faith. For this reason, this mode ought to be the standard practice of the church.

Controversies surrounding baptism have resulted in a tendency to minimize the importance of the ordinance. Some Christian groups do not view baptism as a prerequisite for church membership. Yet New Testament precedence indicates that in all cases baptism is to be administered prior to inclusion in the church. A sincere attempt ought to be made to utilize immersion, even in rare emergency situations. In no such extreme case, however, should the emphasis on immersion as the best mode result in a decision to dispense with baptism entirely.

Baptism and Christian Fellowship

Although believer's baptism, which linked the ordinance to conversion, apparently was the practice of the first-century church, the majority of Christians have been and continue to be sprinkled in infancy. Baptism is generally separated from conversion both logically and temporally. This has confronted Baptists with the continuing problem concerning Christian fellowship—how to relate to believers in the wider Christian community.

There are two "classic" answers to this question. The first suggests that believer's baptism is a definitive mark of the true church. This view implies that any person who belongs to a congregation which generally practices infant baptism is not a member of a true church and therefore does not participate in Christ's body. The second answer suggests that the true church is quite independent of the ecclesiastical bodies present in the world, consisting instead of the entire company of the redeemed, regardless of church affiliation or lack of the same. Entrance into the true church, it is suggested, comes by means of personal conversion, which is viewed solely as an individual, inward event, with baptism as more or less a matter of personal preference or local congregational polity. In this way Christian fellowship is allowed with individuals who are members of congregations with which one's own congregation has no formal fellowship and who have not been baptized according to one's own criterion. To accomplish this, the New Testament understanding of baptism is often diluted and the ordinance itself minimized.

A Baptist response to the issue of fellowship with other Christians ought not to compromise the New Testament emphases on baptism and on the close relationship of this ordinance to conversion and church membership, a compromise often found in modern denominationalism. The experience of conversion begins with the personal desire to belong to Christ (repentance and inward faith) but remains incomplete until this desire comes to fruition in baptism and church membership. At the same time, however, Baptist exclusivism ought be avoided. This is possible when people give place to God's grace, which overflows to humanity in spite of sin and error.

5 The Lord's Supper— The Repeated Ordinance

In addition to baptism, the church as a whole has observed a second sacred practice throughout its history. This rite has had various designations, each one based on some aspect of its significance. Among these are "Eucharist" (arising from the Greek word "to give thanks"), which stresses this event as a thanksgiving celebration, and "Communion," which emphasizes the fellowship experienced among the participants and between them and the risen Lord. Baptists have tended to prefer the term "the Lord's Supper." This designation finds its source in the link between the church ordinance and the meals which Jesus shared with others, especially the final Passover meal he celebrated with his disciples prior to his death.

In contrast to baptism, which as the initiatory ordinance allows for only one actual participation by a believer, this act calls for repeated and regular observance. Yet, although Christians participate in the Lord's Supper weekly, monthly, or quarterly, the presence of many is often motivated only by force of habit, without full awareness of the deep meaning that the ordinance entails.

The Significance of the Lord's Supper Celebration

The New Testament documents stand as clear testimony to the fact that the early Christians held the Lord's Supper in high esteem, because they saw in this rite an act of deep significance. There are perhaps five basic, interdependent themes concerning the significance of this meal in the New Testament. First, the Lord's Supper is significant as proclamation (1 Corinthians 11:26). Similar to baptism, this ordinance is a visual sermon which proclaims the fact and meaning of Jesus' death. The breaking of the bread visually represents the sacrifice of the Lord's body for our sake ("This is my body given for you"). The fruit of the vine poured out visually speaks of the shedding of Jesus' blood for the sins of the world (Hebrews 9:22; Mark 14:24). Because part of the symbolic significance lies in the acts of breaking and pouring, these ought to occur, as far as is practical, during the actual worship service in full view of all participants. The Communion elements ought not to be totally prepared in advance, as is so often the case. Similarly, the very acts of eating and drinking carry high symbolic importance, for they speak of the personal aspect of Christ's sacrifice—"He died for me."

Second, the Lord's Supper is significant as a recalling of Jesus' death. The ordinance is a visual way of repeatedly placing before the community the memory of Jesus of Nazareth in faithfulness to his command, "Do this in remembrance of me." Because of this, the celebration becomes an appropriate occasion for recounting the events of his earthly life, climaxing in his death. Associated with this and as our response to Christ's work, this celebration is Eucharist, that is, an expression of thanksgiving to God for the salvation which has been made available to us (hence Paul's reference to the cup of Thanksgiving in 1 Corinthians 10:16a).

Third, the Lord's Supper is significant in that it is a symbolic participation in Christ (1 Corinthians 10:16). In this context the eating and drinking are once again of great importance. On the one hand, these acts of ingestion are symbols of personal faith. These physical acts, which are the means to the reception of physical nourishment for physical vitality, declare that reception of Christ is crucial for spiritual vitality. Similarly, just as the staples of life, represented by the bread and the fruit of the vine, must be taken into the body and made a part of it for the sustaining of physical life, so also must the reality of Christ be taken into ourselves and made a part of our very being for continued spiritual vitality. These acts, then, symbolize our faith in Christ and his atoning work as the source of spiritual life.

On the other hand, the significance of the eating and drinking must be understood within the context of loyalty to Christ as opposed to loyalty to idols. This emphasis lies behind Paul's statement to the church in Corinth (1 Corinthians 10:16-21). The apostle stresses that participation in the elements at the Lord's Table constitutes a confession of personal allegiance and therefore includes a demand for separation from and renunciation of all idolatrous allegiances. In this way, the Lord's Supper becomes a repeated affirmation of personal commitment to Jesus as Lord, an affirmation which is symbolized by presence at his table and by the acts of eating and drinking those physical elements which symbolize his life.

Fourth, the ordinance is an expression of the unity of the church of Christ (1 Corinthians 10:17). The Lord's Supper cannot be celebrated in isolation but requires the presence of a believing community. At this event, however, all members of the community partake from one loaf, which is a symbolic representation that the corporate group, though consisting of many individuals, remains nevertheless one organism. This meaning of the ordinance is even more poignant when seen within the context of the divisive Corinthian congregation. All schism and every unreconciled conflict is denounced as grievous sin by this act.

Finally, the Lord's Supper is significant as a reminder of the future return of Jesus (1 Corinthians 11:26). This meaning arises out of Jesus' own promise, "I will not drink again of the fruit of the vine until I drink anew with you in the kingdom of God" (Matthew 26:29). Each time the community of faith eats and drinks without gazing upon Christ physically present, testimony is given to the coming day when God's rule will be complete on earth and faith will become sight.

The Importance of the Lord's Supper Celebration

Because the New Testament church saw deep significance in the Lord's Supper, it is not surprising that great emphasis was placed on its observance, an emphasis which has always been present in the church. The value or importance of the continual celebration of this ordinance may be sketched by three considerations. First, we ought to observe this rite because of a desire to be obedient to the Lord. As an ordinance, a practice ordained by Jesus, its observance is a means to symbolize our obedience to him as Lord. Second, the Lord's Supper ought to be observed because of its value as a means of proclaiming the gospel. Christians present at the celebration are given a vivid reminder of Jesus' life and death for them and of his imminent return in glory and judgment. Others present, who are able only to observe the administration of the ordinance, become witnesses to a powerful, visual recounting of the gospel story and thereby are challenged to respond to Jesus' call to conversion. Third, the value in the continual observance of the ordinance lies in the reaffirmation of personal faith in and loyalty to Jesus as Lord, which is entailed in participation in the bread and the cup.

The regular observance of the Lord's Supper within the context of faith is valuable as a channel used by the Holy Spirit. Through participation in the Lord's Supper the believer is strengthened by the Spirit as personal allegiance to Christ is reaffirmed. The Spirit may use the vivid picture of the example of Jesus to admonish the disciple to imitate our Leader. By symbolizing the personal appropriation of spiritual vitality, the act underscores the necessity of continual reliance on the Lord through his Spirit. And through the reminder of Jesus' return embodied in this rite, the Holy Spirit calls the believer to steadfastness, hope, and diligence during the interim period. For others who view the observance of the Lord's Supper the act becomes the vivid illustration of the spoken gospel proclamation, which the Holy Spirit can utilize in convicting persons of their need and in calling those persons to respond to Christ.

Participation in the Lord's Supper Observance

From the remarks made thus far it naturally follows that participation at the Lord's Table must be limited to Christians. Others ought to be welcomed as nonparticipating observers but their actual participation, in the absence of personal faith, could carry no personal significance. Only a believer can give full expression to that which presence at the Lord's Table signifies.

In addition, participation in the initiatory ordinance ought to precede participation in the repeated ordinance, as nearly all Christian faith groups teach. This requirement is based on the nature of baptism and the Lord's Supper. As has been suggested already, these observances are given to the people of God partly as a means to express loyalty to Christ. In this context baptism constitutes a first public affirmation of allegiance, whereas the Lord's Supper expresses a reaffirmation of one's personal commitment. Similarly, baptism precedes the Lord's Supper in that it is the symbol marking the beginning of one's Christian pilgrimage, whereas the latter rite symbolizes the importance of continual appropriation of the Savior's provision for Christian living.

While the Lord's Supper is open to believers only, it is to be open to all believers present who choose to participate. This is based on two considerations. First, the name of the ordinance itself implies this stance. Since it is the Lord's Table and not that of any one particular church or congregation, the Lord himself is the one who is inviting his disciples to join in fellowship. Second, the openness of the celebration is based on the injunction of Paul that each engage in self-examination (1 Corinthians 11:28). Since no other person is in a position to see into the heart of any would-be participant, the decision concerning fellowship at the Lord's Table is a responsibility of the individual, who in turn carries the accountability for any decision made. The task of the officiant in this context is that of issuing the invitation on the Lord's behalf and of reminding those present of the Lord's requirements, which in turn demand serious personal reflection (1 Corinthians 11:27-32).

This principle is applicable in situations in which persons sprinkled in infancy are present. Although baptism is prerequisite to participation in the Lord's Supper each is responsible to determine before God one's own baptized status. The one who in good conscience is convinced of the validity of a baptism administered in infancy ought to be welcomed at the Lord's Table fellowship, even by those who cannot in good conscience personally accept infant baptism.

Self-examination prior to the Lord's Supper ought to be taken seriously. The would-be participant must, of course, be clear concerning personal conversion and baptism. In addition, however, self-examination must include introspection. Participation by any believer in those elements which draw attention to the death of Jesus for the sin of humanity and which symbolize the unity of the church ought to be preceded by confession of sin and reconciliation with all other persons, as far as is possible.

The Presence of Christ at the Lord's Supper

Most Baptists are aware that baptism has been the subject of heated debate during the last several centuries. However, many find surprising that of the two ordinances it is actually the Lord's Supper which has caused the most controversy among Christians and which remains today the greater source of division within the church as a whole. The question around which much of the controversy has revolved is that of the nature of Christ's presence in the celebration of the Eucharist.

Beginning in the Middle Ages the term transubstantiation has been utilized by theologians in the Roman Catholic tradition to suggest that the actual physical body of the Lord is present and ingested at the Eucharist, in that the elements of bread and wine are changed into Christ's body and blood. This interpretation was rejected by the Reformers, who nevertheless differed among themselves as to the correct understanding of this Christian mystery. Luther suggested that the actual physical presence of the risen Lord is found *with* the elements, so that the participant receives Christ's body and blood, not instead of bread and wine as in Catholic thinking, but with the physical symbols. Calvin held that Christ was uniquely present in the Eucharist, not in a physical sense as Lutherans and Catholics taught, but in a spiritual sense. Finally the Zurich leader, Huldreich Zwingli, believed that Christ's presence was not to be found in the elements at all, but rather in the believing community. For him, in contrast to the others, the Lord's Supper is best understood as a memorial meal, commemorating the death of the Lord, and not an eating and drinking of the Lord's body and blood. The view of Zwingli has been the most widely held opinion among Baptists in England and North America, who have reacted against what they have seen as the magical/mysterious understanding of the sacraments found in other traditions.

The debates of the sixteenth century are not dealt with directly in the New Testament and are perhaps even foreign to the thinking of the early church. Yet, it is probable that first-century Christians did view the Lord's Supper as a memorial meal, although one which is similar in intent to the Jewish Passover. As the Jewish Passover depicted the Exodus, so this ordinance depicts the great act of God in Christ. This act is symbolically reenacted so that the community may not only recall God's action in the past but also be reminded of God's continuing presence and God's promises for the future. Therefore, care must be given so that the full significance which the New Testament places in the celebration is allowed to motivate, enliven, and energize contemporary observances of this sacred practice.

III The Polity of The Church

6 Membership in the Church

Although estimates suggest that the majority of North Americans are members of some religious body, many persons, regardless of denomination, view religious affiliation as little more than a cultural formality. Participation in the covenant community is significant, however. It is a rich privilege that links the contemporary believer with those of like faith throughout history. It likewise carries a grave responsibility, for it signifies an abiding covenant with the everlasting God and with God's people everywhere.

The Significance of Church Membership

Membership in a local congregation was less formal in the first century than it is in many Baptist churches today. No formal application/reception process including the giving of testimonies and the voting of the entire membership was apparently utilized, following Peter's Pentecost sermon (Acts 2:41.) Letters of commendation, not too dissimilar from the letters of transfer currently used, were, however, carried from one locale to another. Nevertheless, today's procedures are largely the outgrowth of historical developments since the first century, including the heightening emphasis on initiation rites, which began to occur as early as the late second century, and the proliferation of denominations, which has come into being since the Reformation.

At the same time church membership was in some ways held in greater esteem and seen to be more significant in the early church than today. In contrast to the contemporary stress on the individual, the concepts of belonging and community were emphasized in ancient cultures. The people of God in the biblical era quite naturally viewed the individual Christian in terms of incorporation in the larger whole (e.g., Acts 8:14-17; Romans 15:26-27; Acts 18:24-27). This understanding was underscored by Paul who declared that each Christian is an integral part of all others and stands in need of the contribution of all others (e.g., 1 Corinthians 12:13ff.).

Since the corporate community of faith was seen as the sphere of God's unique presence in the world, exclusion from a congregation of the Lord was taken seriously. Exclusion constituted more than the formal striking of a formerly active member from the church roll. This action meant excommunication from the church of Jesus Christ and being placed once again in that domain in which Satan held sway (1 Corinthians 1-5). So complete was this action that actual excommunication was to result: the excluded person was to be treated by the faithful as an outsider (Matthew 18:17; 1 Corinthians 5:11).

There are certain similarities between the understanding held by the early Christians and that of our forebears in the Congregationalist-Baptist tradition. The English Puritan Separatists came to see the local congregation as a company formed and maintained by a corporate covenant with God. Church membership, therefore, received deep significance because it constituted membership in a covenanted people. Exclusion was treated seriously, since it meant being cut off from the covenant. Unfortunately, the corporate understanding is often lost in our day, due in part to the widely held view that church affiliation is an option to be discussed after an individual's conversion, which alone is seen as crucial for one's eternal status before God. A return to the older, more biblical emphasis would be a step toward renewal in the church.

This understanding of the church as the covenant community poses the question concerning the proper members of that body. At this point Baptists part company with many other Christian groups. Although nearly all Christians are in agreement that baptism is the initiatory observance and important as a sign of entrance into the community, groups that practice infant baptism readily suggest that persons can in some sense be members of the church from their earliest infancy. Baptists, in contrast, hold that church membership, which cannot precede baptism, is limited to those who make a conscious profession of faith that includes baptism. This Baptist viewpoint seeks to uphold a significant Reformed principle, regenerate church membership, which declares that membership in the covenant community properly belongs only to those who give evidence of regeneration (or election).

In contrast to this, some church groups suggest that church membership is for the regenerate and their children (who are to give subsequent evidence of election). It is this understanding of church membership which constitutes a major argument for infant baptism among certain churches of the Reformed tradition. Roman Catholics and Lutherans have tended to suggest that infants who are baptized are in some sense regenerated at the time of baptism, either because of that act (Catholic) or in correspondence with it (Lutheran), and therefore are eligible for inclusion in the church. Despite lengthy theological attempts to justify the presence of infants on church membership lists, Baptists see their own view as validated biblically, theologically, and practically.

In the Baptist context, uniting with the local congregation, which is the visible expression of the church of Jesus Christ, should be viewed as the final step in the process of initiation into the company of the people of God. This process begins with the point of personal faith in Christ as Savior and Lord, is given public expression in water baptism, and comes to completion in church membership. This act, however, must never be viewed as similar to joining a club or organization, for it is the sealing of a covenant with God and with like-minded, "like-committed" persons to walk together as God's people and Jesus' disciples.

The initiatory process into the body of Christ comes about through the action of three parties. It consists of a human aspect (repentance and faith), a divine aspect (regeneration by the Holy Spirit), and a churchly aspect (baptism and church membership). These three aspects ought to be viewed together, much the same as in conversion itself. Significant for conversion are the action of God upon the individual, that person's own response to God, and the work of God through the corporate community. In a similar way the triad of inward faith, its outward expression in baptism, and the believer's incorporation into the local congregation belong together.

Membership Procedures

The membership procedures adopted by a local congregation should express a proper understanding of the nature of the church and the significance of church membership. The themes of "covenant" and "interdependence" ought to be especially evident. As an outgrowth of such principles, Baptists have generally accepted persons into their congregations by three means. First, personal confession of faith expressed in baptism is the norm for new believers. In this case the ordinance constitutes the act through which the individual seals his or her covenant with God, and the ordinance administered in the context of the church followed by the "right hand of fellowship" denotes the mutual covenant between convert and congregation.

Second, those who have been baptized and who hold membership elsewhere are received by transfer of membership. In this case, the receiving congregation requests by formal correspondence a letter of recommendation from the believer's former church. This act entails a relinquishing of the former covenant in order that a covenant can be sealed between the disciple and the community of faith which that person is desiring to join.

A third procedure, reception by restoration, is used in the situation of a person who has been excluded from fellowship and now wishes to be reinstated by the excluding body or received by some other congregation. This act constitutes a reowning of a covenant formerly made. If the exclusion had been undertaken by a congregation elsewhere, care must be given to insure that the underlying causes of that action have been alleviated and any necessary restitution has been made before admitting to fellowship. Communication with the former congregation is imperative in all such situations. A variation of this procedure involves receiving by Christian experience a believer who having been inactive was erased from the membership of a congregation elsewhere.

Since local church membership entails the forming of a mutual covenant between believers, admittance of new persons to the congregation is the prerogative of the entire body, though it is generally expedient to allow the congregation's spiritual leaders to function in an advisory capacity. The personal testimony of each candidate ought to be heard by this group and preferably by the entire congregation prior to acceptance. Formal membership in turn should commence with appropriate expressions of welcome by the pastor (or moderator) as church representative ("the hand of fellowship") and by the body as a whole (e.g., informal words of welcome and support).

Termination of membership generally occurs either by transfer to another congregation or by death. Unfortunately, situations do arise which call for termination by a third means, exclusion, even in congregations which seriously seek to encourage and admonish one another. New Testament grounds for exclusion include departure from the faith (1 Timothy 1:18-20), unrepentant immoral living (1 Corinthians 5:1-11), and an unreconciling spirit (Matthew 18:15-18). Exclusion is necessary when all other courses of action have been exhausted in the attempt to assist the offending party in rectifying the problem (Matthew 18:15-18; Galatians 6:1-2). When exclusion is unavoidable, action must be undertaken in a spirit of love and with a sense of deep sorrow, knowing the spiritual significance of the act, and with the sincere desire that the exclusion of the member will result in future restoration (e.g., 2 Corinthians 2:5-11). Serious attention must be given to prayer at all stages, and supplication for the excluded one ought to continue even after church action is completed.

Some suggest a fourth means of termination, erasure, in the case of one who indicates no interest in the church for an extended period of time. While nonresident members are a special category, disinterested resident members are in violation of New Testament precedent and command (Acts 2:42-47; Hebrews 10:24-25). Such persons ought to be reminded of their covenant obligations. In cases of continued disinterest, steps toward exclusion, rather than mere erasure, are generally appropriate due to the seriousness of this situation.

At all times it must be remembered that the goal of church discipline in any of its forms is reconciliation, not punishment. Discipline, therefore, must always be motivated by loving concern for the wayward member and be carried out in the context of genuine grieving over the need for such action (1 Corinthians 5:2). Once discipline has produced repentance and reconciliation, the disciplined member ought to receive the fellowship and support of the entire congregation (2 Corinthians 2:7-11).

7 Government of the Church

Paul suggested to the Christians in Rome that civil government is present in society by divine design for the benefit of humanity (Romans 13:1-7). The church, like secular society, has found governmental structure beneficial. Church government is one important means of organizing the people of God for the task entrusted to them. In the Baptist tradition government centers on the local congregation and the wider association.

Government of the Church as a Whole

Among the issues dividing the various ecclesiastical traditions, one which is immensely practical is the question as to how the church as a whole is to be governed. Three major options find significant following in our contemporary situation: the hierarchical, the representative, and the congregational. The hierarchical system suggests that authority in the church flows from Christ through a select group of persons (e.g., bishops) to the individual congregations. Local congregations are in turn seen as being a part of the church insofar as they are "in fellowship with" (or come under the authority of) a member of this mediating group.

The second model of church government is the representative type. In this system the church is governed by a synod consisting of persons who have been elected to this task by various congregations. These local congregations come under the authority of the external body but, nevertheless, have a voice in determining the composition of that group.

In contrast to both these systems the congregational model declares that each local body derives its authority directly from the risen Lord, who alone is the head of the church. Each congregation is autonomous, that is, responsible under Christ for its own affairs. Such congregations ought to band together in associations, but associational authority is largely advisory, rather than legislative, and generally requires the concurrence of the local body. The congregational model has traditionally been practiced by Baptist churches.

This fundamental difference in church government is reflected in the very names of the various denominations. Whereas most groups speak of a national or international church (e.g., the Presbyterian Church), Baptists generally employ terms such as "conference" or "convention" of churches. There is no Baptist Church, only Baptist churches, many suggest.

Some would claim that all models of church government are equally valid since the roots of all of them are found within the apostolic church. There is, however, significant data in the New Testament to indicate that the congregational model was widely practiced, even to the extent of overshadowing all others, and this perhaps by theological design. The book of Acts, for example, indicates that individual congregations made important decisions apart from external coercion (e.g., Acts 13:1-4). Even the Jerusalem Council, which exerted some authority over the various local bodies, was constituted in part by messengers voluntarily sent from at least one local congregation, namely, that in Antioch (Acts 15:23). Similarly, Paul admonished the Corinthian church to take charge of its own affairs—to address the problem of internal schism (1 Corinthians 1:10), to assume jurisdiction for the proper observance of the Lord's Supper (1 Corinthians 11:33-34), and to act to preserve the purity of church membership by means of excommunication (1 Corinthians 5:3-5, 12-13). These considerations constitute a basis for continuing the practice of congregational autonomy.

Local congregational autonomy must never be equated with congregational individualism. Rather, interdependency is clearly the norm in the New Testament. The decision of the council at Jerusalem was intended to be accepted by churches and persons on all sides of the controversy. Likewise, local groups were called to acknowledge a certain authority which the Lord invested in his apostles. Apostolic representatives, such as Timothy and Titus, and other officers were to be received in a special way. Paul himself appealed to what was practiced in all churches as carrying a degree of authority (1 Corinthians 11:16; 14:33). In all matters, the fundamental oneness of all congregations as the one people of God was to be kept in view.

Baptists have sought to preserve both congregational autonomy and intercongregational dependency by stressing the autonomy of the local congregation within an associational framework. According to this view each congregation is self-governing and possesses "church powers"—power of membership (inclusion and exclusion), power of mandate (mobilization of its membership for worship, edification, and outreach), and power of organization (selection of officers—Acts 6:1-5; ordination—Acts 13:1-4; 1 Timothy 4:14). Each congregation, however, is also voluntarily united with other congregations in an associational framework for the purpose of advice, fellowship, and combining resources for the completion of the task common to the entire people of God.

In addition to many practical advantages, the participation of a local, autonomous congregation in various voluntary associations carries important theological significance. Local, regional, national, and international organizations established and maintained by joint congregational efforts, whether directly or indirectly through denominations, all serve to give expression to the reality of the wider Christian fellowship. Each local church is to be the church of Jesus Christ in miniature and as such is self-governing. Yet, this does not suggest that each one is to be a church of Jesus Christ in isolation. Cooperation with other congregations through associational ties at various levels, when understood in this light, becomes the product of the local church's striving to participate in that whole of which it is such a significant part.

Associational Councils

Using the example of the Jerusalem Council as a basis, Baptist congregations call together associational councils to advise local congregations in various situations. The most common type is the ordination council, which is discussed in chapter nine. Two others, however, are also common. A church recognition council is called when a new congregation is seeking associational membership, as has been mentioned in chapter two. Similarly, an ordination recognition council convenes in order to assist in the case of a person whose ordination is in question. Although Baptist ordination is usually accepted by any Baptist congregation, recognition of non-Baptist ordination is not automatic. In the latter case, the council seeks to determine both the soundness of the ordination in question and the extent to which the ordained person's convictions are compatible with Baptist understandings. The council's recommendation to the church does not pertain to subsequent ordination, but to recognition of a prior act completed elsewhere. If the advisory body is satisfied with the credentials and convictions of the one whose ordination is under review, a recognition/installation service, hosted by the local congregation, should be scheduled.

Three other types of councils are occasionally needed to assist with severe local problems. A church which is deeply divided over a significant issue may call a council for assistance. Excluded member(s) councils are called to mediate grievances between individuals and the congregation. A council is also to be called when the congregation senses that the ordination of one serving among them ought to be revoked. In each of these cases, the local area minister ought to be contacted at an early stage and a council called only with that person's concurrence.

Government Within the Churches

The roots of the modern Baptist understanding of the church and its polity lie in the Congregationalists among the sixteenth-century English Puritans, who claimed that each local congregation ought to be self-governing. They also concerned themselves with the proper governance of the local congregation, declaring that the will of Christ for his church is to be discerned by the entire company guided by their leaders, a revolutionary understanding in a day when kings and synods decided the will of God. But the Congregationalists were divided as to the outworking of this principle in the actual local situation. Some came to practice what is called semi-presbyterianism, which saw the final authority in the local church as residing with the local elders, and not with the people as a whole.

Others attempted to apply the same democratic tendency present in the concept of the autonomy of the local congregation to the internal governing of each local church by following a model which is referred to as "democratic congregationalism." This view declares that the final authority in the church resides in the entire membership. Leaders are selected to teach and to guide, but they do not become a governing body over the members themselves. In this model it is the congregation meeting together which is to handle the affairs of the church, seeking corporately the will of Christ, under the guidance of its leaders.

Baptists have generally professed adherence to the principle of democratic congregationalism, because it forms a natural outworking of a great Protestant hallmark, the priesthood of all believers. This biblical concept resurfaced in the question raised in the Reformation concerning access to God and God's available grace. The Roman Catholic Church of the Middle Ages emphasized the importance of a special clergy class in mediating the grace of God, which the church supposedly dispensed to the people as a whole. The priestly class likewise functioned as mediators of the offerings and prayers of the people to God. In the Reformation the concept of the unmediated access to God available to all believers was rediscovered. Because of the work of one Mediator, all believers, and not merely the clergy, were seen as priests. Baptists, following the radical Congregationalists, worked out the implications of this doctrine for the governance of the church.

The priesthood of all believers is a significant New Testament concept, arising out of at least four considerations. First, the New Testament does indeed speak of all believers as being priests (1 Peter 2:5; Revelation 1:6; 5:10; 20:6).. Second, all have the privilege of approaching God (Hebrews 4:15-16; 10:19-20). Third, no mediatory hierarchy is to exist among the followers of Christ (Matthew 23:8-12; 1 Timothy 2:5; Mark 10:42-44). Finally, each believer has the duty of performing the priestly functions of offering sacrifices to God (Hebrews 13:15; Romans 12:1; 1 Peter 2:9) and interceding for others (1 Timothy 2:1-2; 2 Thessalonians 3:1; James 5:16).

Believer priesthood is expressed in the life of the church in various ways. Each member is to be actively functioning in a priestly way in the corporate body according to that person's own gifts. The mandate of the church, whether worship, edification, or outreach, is a common responsibility, and not merely that of a special class. Decisions concerning the affairs of the church are to be matters for the concern of all, not just a few. In the same way leaders are to be selected and pastors ordained by processes in which the entire membership plays a role. Since each believer has been gifted for ministry within the context of the body of Christ (1 Corinthians 12:7), the preparation of the members for service is to be a significant goal of pastoral activity (Ephesians 4:12).

Unfortunately in many Baptist circles democratic congregationalism is diluted or abandoned outright. Some have slipped into a modern-day type of semi-presbyterianism in which the clergy dominates or a select few rule. In some cases a strong pastor makes all major decisions. In other cases the congregation is constitutionally divested of its right to select church leaders. Democratic congregationalism is diluted whenever congregational decisions are reached by means of "politicking" within the membership or when church members simply abdicate their responsibility to be concerned, active participants in the life of the church. This latter situation is noticeable in the trend toward reduced quorum requirements for church business meetings. Except when faced with items of great controversy, many congregations do well if a small minority are present to conduct church business.

Democratic congregationalism has also been open to misunderstanding. Often the "democratic" aspect is interpreted in the sense of rule by majority. Actually, however, this principle has reference to the active role of all in the corporate search for the will of Christ for the church. True democratic congregationalism is the discerning of the will of Christ by the entire body under the guidance of its leaders, and not the rule by a select few nor by the voting majority at meagerly attended church meetings.

The implementation of democratic congregationalism requires that church leaders understand their God-given responsibilities of equipping the members for the task of corporate discernment by means of teaching, informing, and guiding, in order that enlightened decisions can be made. It also requires that church members shoulder their responsibility to be active, spiritual, informed, and conscientious partners in the ministry of the congregation. In this way church meetings can become what they were intended to be, community attempts to search out together what the Spirit is saying, rather than the gathering of a few to air and vote their own personal preferences.

Procedures for Congregational Meetings

A correct understanding of the nature, purpose, and governance of the church ought to affect the way in which congregational meetings are conducted. The purpose of these gatherings as occasions for the people of God to determine the mind of Christ for his people serves as a guide to the types of topics to be included on the meeting agenda. In general, matters that have significant bearing on the welfare and ministry of the church as a whole ought to be the concern of the entire congregation. Such matters include selection of pastoral staff, election of church officers, adoption of church budget, decisions concerning the major property or programming changes, reception of new members, enactment of disciplinary measures, and issuance of letters of transfer. In addition to transacting routine business, the church body should utilize the congregational meeting to explore how it can best fulfill its mission to the community in which it is located.

The effectiveness of the church meeting is heightened when preliminary discussions transpire within the various committees and boards. In this way the leadership is given opportunity to provide initial guidance, and specific, detailed proposals can be formulated to facilitate the deliberations of the total body. Church committees form proper forums also for decisions of lesser magnitude and for matters not germane to the work of the congregation as a whole.

A proper understanding of church government should likewise determine how church meetings are to be conducted, with the goal of facilitating corporate discernment of the will of the Lord always being uppermost. To this end, some system of order must be adopted. One widely used system, *Robert's Rules of Order,* makes provision for broad involvement in decision making in an orderly fashion through the use of means such as the formal motion, discussion, and voting. But any system must be tempered by the desire for broad consensus rather than strict majority rule and by an emphasis on seeking and speaking the words of Christ rather than simply expressing personal preferences (1 Peter 4:11a).

Crucial to the success of church meetings is the selection of a capable moderator, who, because of knowledge of leadership techniques, is able to direct the flow of the meeting in an orderly fashion. It is generally preferable that the pastor not serve in this capacity. Further, having the moderator also chair the church board allows for greater continuity between board discussions and church decision making. Because board and congregational decisions carry significance well into the future, official records ought to be kept in the form of "minutes." The task of recording and retaining the minutes should be entrusted to a capable person selected by the church.

8 ❧
Offices in the Church

Every believer is to be a priest, actively ministering within the corporate community. But to promote an effective corporate ministry, some degree of organization is needed. Since the first century, the church has employed various office structures for the purpose of providing the community with the leadership of capable persons.

Church Officers in the New Testament Era

In his greeting to the Christians at Philippi, Paul bears witness to the presence in the early local communities of two basic types of offices, "bishop" and "deacon" (cf. Philippians 1:1). The first seems to have been the result of a blending of two somewhat related traditions, the Greek and the Jewish. This is not surprising since the Pauline churches contained members from both backgrounds. From the Greek understanding arose the term bishop (Greek *episkopos*, from which comes the English word "episcopal"), which means "one who supervises or oversees" (see Acts 20:28; 1 Timothy 3:1-2; Titus 1:7).

Jewish synagogue organizational structure is reflected in another term, elder (Greek *presbyteros*, from which arise "presbyter" and "presbyterian"). In the Jewish context elder could refer either to chronological age or special status within the synagogue community. This word was then transferred into the Christian setting (see Acts 20:17; 1 Timothy 5:17-19; Titus 1:5; James 5:14; 1 Peter 5:1ff.). It is likely that bishop and elder are actually alternate designations for what was essentially one office, since both terms are used interchangeably in some contexts (elder in Acts 20:17 and bishop in verse 28; see also Titus 1:5,7).

The New Testament gives some indication as to the functions which the bishops or elders fulfilled. First, the term bishop suggests a supervisory task. These persons were given the responsibility of overseeing the ongoing functioning of the congregation under their care. For this reason they were instructed to "shepherd" or guide (Acts 20:28; 1 Peter 5:2). Likewise, they were involved in coordinating the ministry of the congregation (1 Timothy 3:5; 5:17), providing an administrative leadership which included involvement in that ministry.

Second, it seems that these persons functioned as spiritual leaders for the congregation. Certain spiritual tasks were theirs because of their position (James 5:14). Similarly, preaching, teaching, admonishing, and guarding against heresy were included among their duties (Titus 1:9). Because of the grave responsibilities involved, the office was to be filled only with persons who met strict qualifications (1 Timothy 3:1-7).

The second basic office in the early church was that of deacon or helper. "Deacon" (Greek *diakonos*) is derived from a verb which means "to wait on someone at table" (Luke 12:37), "to minister to the needs of another" (Matthew 4:11; 1 Timothy 1:18) or "to render assistance or support" (Matthew 25:44). Thus, literally a deacon was a table waiter, one who took care of the needs of others, or an assistant.

There is not an abundance of evidence as to how those holding the office of helper functioned in the New Testament church. It appears that the first impetus to the eventual establishment of this office arose in the Jerusalem church. A group was selected to assist the apostles with some of the organizational responsibilities of the congregation, in order that the twelve could be freed to devote more time to their primary function of providing spiritual leadership (Acts 6:1-4). By the time of the writing of the Pastoral Epistles, the office had been established and "helpers" had become an official designation for those serving as assistants to the overseers. These persons perhaps also were apprentices who in turn would eventually become local leaders. Because of the importance of the position, all who were to be appointed as helpers were to be persons who fulfilled certain qualifications (1 Timothy 3:8-12).

These considerations suggest the presence of a two-tiered structure in certain congregations. The local leadership responsibilities were shared by a group of persons, called bishops or elders (the New Testament generally uses the plural form when referring to holders of this office). This leadership was to be exercised for the benefit of the entire congregation. Assisting these leaders was another group of people, helpers or assistants, who were "in training" but who also took care of some of the lesser administrative tasks.

In addition to these local congregational officers there were other persons in the early church whose influence and authority transcended the boundary of the single local congregation. One such office was that of apostle. Paul, for example, claimed a certain amount of authority, which he continually struggled to defend in the face of rebellious elements in the churches to which he wrote. Likewise, in his first epistle John declares that one mark of all true churches is doctrinal purity, that is, loyalty to apostolic authority and teaching.

A second example of a group of persons whose authority went beyond any one congregation is that of the apostolic assistants, who acted as emissaries of the apostles and who therefore shared in their authority. Titus and Timothy stand as two important examples. On at least one occasion Titus was called upon to appoint leaders for a group of local congregations (Titus 1:5), a task which Paul had earlier fulfilled in a similar context (Acts 14:23). Whether this was accomplished by means of supervised elections (as some claim) or by personal selection, the implication is the same; authority was exercised by someone whose official status was not limited to the particular local body.

The most significant and interesting example for the modern situation is that of pastor/teacher. This office was linked by Paul with those of apostle, prophet, and evangelist in a short list of Christ's gifts to his church (Ephesians 4:11-12). Here, the church in general and not any specific congregation is in view, indicating that such persons carry a certain authority in the church as a whole. In the first century apostles were responsible for the articulation, proclamation, and maintainance of foundational doctrine. Prophets and evangelists carried on itinerant work, using churches established by apostles as a basis of ministry. Pastors and teachers, it appears, were those who worked within a specific locale for an extended period of time in order to edify the congregation by their ministry.

Timothy is often seen as the best example of an early pastor. Tradition suggests that after serving as Paul's assistant, he was sent to the Ephesian church, where he remained for an extended time. This Ephesian sojourn formed the background for the writing of the two Timothy letters. Timothy's career, coupled with Paul's statement in Ephesians 4, constitutes a basis for the understanding of the pastoral office today as one which centers on ministry within the context of a local congregation, but which has ramifications beyond the local setting.

Church Officers in the Contemporary Situation

Until the nineteenth century, church structure among Baptists in America was quite simple. Whenever possible, local congregations sought out a gifted person to fulfill various pastoral duties, including preaching and evangelism, although such a one was generally referred to as elder rather than pastor. Assisting the ordained elder were a group of laypersons, called deacons, who administered the more mundane church affairs. Associational structure was likewise simple. Member congregations appointed messengers to attend regularly scheduled associational business sessions. Leadership for association projects was often provided by the elders serving member congregations, although assistance from neighboring associations was sometimes utilized.

The nineteenth century was an era of change in Baptist life as the movement entered the religious mainstream. Congregations grew in size, acquired property, added new programs, and became legally incorporated. Pastors became better educated and more mobile. These changes resulted in more complex church structures. Locally, additional boards—trustees, Christian education—were added to administer the expanded programs and facilities, and the office of deacon took on the task of concern for "the spiritual well-being" of the congregation. The pastor was often assisted in the administration of the more complex structure by a church board, consisting of representatives from the various committees.

On the interchurch level, national bodies developed. As cooperative programming expanded, needs arose for full-time persons to administer the activities of the denomination, which, because of the scope, diversity, and size of these endeavors, could no longer be maintained by groups of local pastors alone.

Baptists today rightfully understand the pastor as one sent by the Lord into a specific congregation for service to that body for an indefinite period of time. Yet, the significance of the office is not limited to that one body. In addition to the primary role within the local congregation the pastoral office generally carries a somewhat informal authority within both the wider civic community of residence and the wider ecclesiastical arena of association, denomination, and church as a whole.

Within the local setting itself the pastor is to function within the framework of the local leaders. At the same time the pastor's ministry is one of greater depth because of the "full-time" status involved therein. The scope of pastoral responsibilities is indicated by the injunctions to Timothy in the epistles which bear his name. The general functions of the elders, such as "shepherding" and leading worship, are augmented by other more specialized duties including teaching, preaching, and evangelism. All of this is to be done in light of an ultimate objective, namely, preparing the people of God for work of the ministry given to the church of Christ (see Ephesians 4:11ff.). In other words, the pastor in the local congregation is an elder;

yet the special call and the greater task suggest that each pastor is more than merely an elder.

The pastoral office is also present on the associational/denominational level. All pastors of member congregations are implicitly entrusted with an informal authority, because of the local leadership which they provide. In addition, however, explicit authority is entrusted by associational groups to persons such as denominational officials, area ministers, and teaching faculty. These associational offices are extensions of the pastoral office, for such persons provide pastoral ministry and generally carry pastoral ordination. But the pastoral role here is definitely intercongregational in scope, since a constituency wider than any one local body forms the selecting and delegating body and becomes the object of the ministry of such persons.

Office structures are not ends in themselves but only a means through which the Holy Spirit seeks to provide capable leadership to the community for the fulfillment of its task. Each congregation ought to develop a structure under the Spirit's guidance which best meets its own needs. With this in mind one specific model for local congregational structure will be outlined, which serves as an example of a way in which the form that eventually took shape in the Pauline churches and the insights gained from the Baptist experience can be incorporated into the contemporary situation. This model shares many similarities with structures currently employed by many Baptist churches. It includes a church board, which has certain affinities with the traditional deacon board. It also includes various committees chaired by church board members, which assume the tasks assigned to boards of trustees, Christian education, and the like. Yet, the model outlined here purposely avoids traditional terminology, such as elder and deacon, since the purely functional connotations which these designations carried in the New Testament (bishop as the coordinating function and deacon as the helper function) have largely been lost in contemporary usage.

At the center of the organizational structure of the local congregation and directly accountable to the body as a whole is the church board (or board of supervisors, overseers, presbyters, elders—the exact name is less important than the function), selected by the congregation and charged with the task of providing spiritual leadership and direction to the church in its program of ministry. The pastor (or pastoral staff) is to be a member of this board, as is the chairperson or moderator of the congregation. The remaining board members should include those persons who are charged with coordinating the various aspects of the mandate given to the church; a worship coordinator, an outreach coordinator, and an edification coordinator (responsible for Christian education and nurture) are examples. Larger churches may find it advantageous to divide the edification ministry, establishing separate coordinators for education and nurture. Since resources are needed for the completion of the mandate, there ought to be a resources coordinator (finance, buildings) on the board as well. What is of highest significance is that each of these persons be entrusted with the task of providing responsible leadership in a specific area of the life of the congregation; thus, each is a functioning leader.

Final authority remains with the congregation as a whole, a principle which is seen even in the selection process. Pastors are called by the entire church for an indefinite term of office. All other members of the church board are likewise determined by action of the congregation, generally selected for a specific length of service. This selection is to be based on stringent criteria: spiritual qualification (1 Timothy 3:1-7), gifts and interest in the specific field of service, and proven effectiveness in other tasks.

Structured under the church board and serving with the members of this board are the various congregational officers which fall in the helper category. These officers may be added according to the sensed needs of the congregation and with the purpose of assisting the board members in carrying out their assigned tasks. Helpers could quite naturally be organized into standing committees in the various areas of church ministry, such as outreach committee, edification committee (or education committee and nurture committee in larger churches), worship committee, resources committee, and the like. Whenever this occurs, the respective coordinator would serve both as committee chairperson and liaison between the committee and the church board. Persons who fill helper functions are given appropriate officer status and committee membership by the congregation (perhaps with the approval of the board), after having met a similar stringent criteria: spiritual qualifications (1 Timothy 3:9-11), gifts and interest in the field of endeavor, and proven effectiveness in other responsibilities. Length of service is also stipulated by congregational prerogative.

The service orientation of all officers, whether intercongregational, pastoral, supervisory, or helper, must never be overlooked. As those chosen by and endowed with special responsibilities by a congregation or group of congregations, these persons have been entrusted with leadership authority. Their positions, however, do not entail license to promote personal, selfish goals, but rather are to be accepted in all humility and with the intent of seeking the good of the whole. This same spirit is to dominate all committee and board meetings as consensus and even unanimity concerning the will of Christ for his church are sought corporately.

Ordination

Most Christian traditions, including the Baptist, ordain pastors and other clergy. The practice of publicly setting aside leaders has its roots in the Bible, in both Israel and the New Testament church. Already in the Old Testament the act of laying on hands, which is widely practiced today in conjunction with ordination, signified in certain cases the investment of a person with leadership responsibility and authority. The book of Numbers, for example, reports that Moses under command of God laid hands on Joshua in the presence of the priest and the community (Numbers 27:18-23).

A significant example of an ordained minister in the early Christian community is Timothy. The New Testament indicates that the ordination of this young companion of Paul was linked to a personal call which he received. His call arose out of a prophetic pronouncement concerning his future role (1 Timothy 1:18; cf. Acts 13:2-3). Subsequent to this came his actual public ordination as one set apart, an event which included the laying on of hands by the elders of a local congregation (1 Timothy 4:14). Hence, in Timothy's ordination two elements were present, a divine call and the confirmation of the local body.

Theological Basis of Ordination

The basis of the practice of ordination lies in certain theological understandings which reflect concerns central to all of Scripture. First, ordination arises ultimately out of God's program in history. The sovereign Creator and Redeemer is at work in history bringing all creation to a climax in the final, eternal rule of the Triune God. Within this program for human history, God sovereignly calls persons to places of service. Certain persons are called to certain special leadership tasks in the program of God. Ordination is the recognition and confirmation by the corporate people of God of the presence of this special call to a particular individual.

Closely linked with this is the ecclesiastical basis for ordination. As has been seen previously, the New Testament refers to certain functions within the body of Christ, which, although related to the local congregation, in some sense transcend the boundaries of any one congregation. The New Testament gives evidence that persons who were to serve in offices such as these were set apart for this service by a public act. This development was anticipated in the action of the Lord himself, for he appointed from among his disciples twelve persons, who were to play a special role in his mission (Mark 3:13-14). The loss of Judas from among this group resulted in an action undertaken by the disciples in the upper room just prior to Pentecost, which added Matthias to the ranks of the twelve (Acts 1:21-23). This public ordaining by the community was their response to the wishes of the Holy Spirit. Later, Barnabas and Paul were ordained in Antioch immediately prior to the commencement of their missionary service (Acts 13:1-3).

In the New Testament era ordination carried a twofold significance. On the one hand, it was related to the gift of the empowering Holy Spirit (1 Timothy 4:14; 2 Timothy 1:6). On the other hand, the act constituted a public commissioning of one of God's servants (Acts 13:3; cf. Numbers 27:18-23). Hence, special officers, who had been selected and endowed by the sovereign Spirit for the performance of special tasks in service to the church, were commissioned by the body of Christ in public acknowledgment of the Spirit's action.

Ordination in a Baptist Context

In the understanding of Baptists and certain other free churches the ordaining body can only be the local congregation. This is based on the priesthood of all believers and the principle that Christ's authority in the church is generally mediated through the local people, rather than through a clergy group. Ordained officers, then, are leaders who have been designated by the people themselves, and not a small hierarchy perpetuating themselves and their power.

Baptist ecclesiology stresses the leadership function of the ordained person. Such a one is called chiefly to lead the people of God in service (Ephesians 4:11-13) and not to be the mediator of God's grace or Christ's will. Therefore, rather than being set in a position over the people, the ordained person stands with them as together they seek to be obedient to the Lord of the church. In addition to serving in a leadership role within the local congregation, an ordained person may also be an extension of the local congregation, just as Barnabas and Paul served as missionary representatives of the Antioch church.

This understanding of the role of the clergy is visible in the actual act of ordination symbolized by the laying on of hands, for this rite is carried out by the local leaders as representatives of the local congregation. Although generally all ordained persons present in the worship service are invited to participate in the ceremony, their participation is designed to give expression to the oneness of the entire church and not to deny the prerogative of the local body in ordination. This same principle is also seen in the calling of the ordination council. Noteworthy is the fact that it is at the discretion of that local congregation that an ordination council is called, and not by decision of a denomination official or a group of pastors. Further, the council technically serves only as an advisory body to the local congregation concerning whether or not to proceed with ordination. Thus, the local congregation is the ordaining body, which is to act with the advice of other churches.

At the same time, however, there is an additional significance in the calling of a council. This action is an outgrowth of the local congregation's desire to act in harmony with sister churches and as such is an expression of the principle of interdependency. In ordaining one of its own, a congregation is acting on behalf of the church as a whole. In calling an advisory council, that congregation acknowledges its responsibility to and its need for the assistance of others. Hence, it is with a profound awareness that no church is an entity to itself that the ordaining congregation calls this council.

At the same time, the calling of the council acknowledges an important fact concerning the nature of ordination itself, namely, that this act transcends the local congregation. Although ordination derives its authority from the local church, the exercise of that authority will go beyond its boundaries. The ordained status will be carried by the candidate to whatever future places of service this person may be called. Likewise, as an ordained person this individual will exercise a certain authority in the denomination, in the entire Christian community, and in society. Therefore, it is important that no local congregation take upon itself the task of ordination apart from the advice of other churches by means of the representative ordination council.

Not only is the ordaining body important, but also the act itself is of significance in the Baptist context. There are three aspects to the meaning of ordination. First, ordination is a recognition that the Holy Spirit has invested this person with certain gifts for ministry. The laying on of hands symbolizes in part the coming of the Holy Spirit on an individual to empower that person for the task to which that one has been called. Second, ordination is an act of commissioning by the church. Through this act the community places a person into a significant area of service within the body of Christ. Third, ordination is a public declaration of ministerial position. In our society clergy status is recognized in the civil sphere as well as the ecclesiastical. In ordination public testimony is given to the fact that the candidate has been entrusted with this position and may be called upon to fulfill whatever functions society relegates to clergy.

The Task of an Ordination Council

In addition to what has already been stated, an overriding basis for the practice of calling a council lies in Paul's injunction against hasty ordination (1 Timothy 5:22). This admonition and the deep significance of this act demand that the local congregation take to heart the solemn nature of the ordination process and not act alone in ordaining a person for pastoral leadership. Out of this concern an advisory council is called. This body serves as a safeguard against ordaining anyone who lacks proper preparation, credentials, or a definite call from the Lord.

The council's main function is that of examining the candidate with respect to soundness for ordination, in order that it might render advice to the ordaining church. This examination should include three areas. First, the candidate is to be examined with respect to a call to the ministry. The council seeks to make determinations, such as: Is this person called of God to this special function within the kingdom of God? Is the candidate able to give testimony to the reception of a divine call and does that experience constitute a legitimate call? Second, the council must examine the candidate concerning soundness of doctrine within the context of the teaching of Christ's church (not necessarily as measured by the specific viewpoint of certain members of the council). Equally important, however, is the candidate's expertise in articulating and supporting personal theological viewpoints, since ordained Christian leaders function as theologians within Christ's church and in society as a whole.

Third, the ordination council should examine the candidate's concept of personal ministry. Here questioning ought to probe philosophy of ministry, understanding of ministry, and direction of personal calling. The candidate ought to be able to articulate clearly the nature of the gospel ministry and have a clear understanding of his or her place in the church. If the person fails in any of these three areas, the advice of the council to the congregation should be to wait with ordination. On the other hand, once satisfied with the candidate's call, doctrinal soundness and theological expertise, and concept of personal ministry, the council is able to concur wholeheartedly with the decision of the church.

Procedure for Ordination

Although there are exceptions, the ordination process generally begins with the growing conviction among the leaders of a local congregation that the reality of God's call is being demonstrated in ministry among them by one who has sensed an inner call and has undergone theological training. The leaders articulate their conviction to the entire congregation, who in turn confirm that conviction by corporate resolve to seek the advice of the association concerning ordination. The candidate's affirmation of faith should be drawn up at this time. This document ought to contain a brief description of the candidate's call to the ministry, convictions in the major areas of Christian doctrine, views on traditional Baptist distinctives, and a personal concept of the ministry.

If the local association has formed a committee on ordination for the purpose of offering preliminary advice to member congregations in the matter of calling ordination councils, it is proper for the church to contact this committee at this point. The committee will then review the candidate's credentials and affirmation of faith, hold an interview (if necessary), and give a recommendation to the church. Should the recommendation be favorable, the congregation then formally requests that each association church send representatives (generally pastor(s) plus two church leaders) to form a council at a prescribed time and location. The candidate's ordination documents should be distributed to the various representatives prior to the scheduled council meeting. It is generally advisable that representation from a minimum of six association churches be present to constitute a council.

Although the council generally meets in the ordaining church's facilities and although members of the ordaining church may wish to be present for the questioning, care ought to be taken by the host church to insure that its role on the council is minimal. Obtaining the advice of other churches is the goal, not convincing the others of the validity of the host congregation's desire to ordain the candidate. To this end the host church ought to limit the size of its representation to that of the other churches (or less).

The council is called to session by a leader of the host church. Organizational matters are then expedited, such as the seating of the delegates and the election of council officers (chairperson and clerk). Sometimes temporary officers are elected first; then they officiate the election of permanent officers. Next, the candidate is introduced and the resolution of the host church is read. The bulk of the time is devoted to the candidate's call, affirmation of faith, and concept of ministry, with the corresponding questioning by council members. The session is climaxed by the deliberations of the council. Since this is a closed session, only council members are to be present at this point. During this session the representatives of the host church are free to express their reactions to the questioning, but it is wise for them to play only a minor role in the actual council deliberations. The council formulates a resolution to the host church and votes on it. Host representatives should abstain from voting if a lack of unanimity is sensed from the discussion. The council resolution is reported to the church. If the advice is favorable, plans for a subsequent ordination service may proceed.

Ordination services vary greatly; yet certain features are generally included. The resolutions of the church body and ordination council may be read. A sermon concerning the nature of ordination or the role(s) of the ordained person is fitting. A charge is given to the candidate, followed by one to the ordaining church, which underscores this congregation's significant future ministry in the life of the one they are setting apart. The high point of the service is the laying on of hands, symbolizing the impartation of authority and the gift of the Spirit for ministry. The local officers, who symbolize the ordaining congregation, plus all ordained clergy present, symbolizing the church as a whole and the interdependency of the churches, are involved in this act.

IV ❀ The Baptist Movement

10. The Genesis of the Modern Baptist Movement

Baptist historians have carried on a lively debate concerning the genesis of the ecclesiastical tradition which bears the name "Baptist." In the nineteenth century a viewpoint was popularized, called Landmarkism, which attempted to forge a chain that would link the Baptists of America back to the New Testament church. The links in this chain included various reform-minded, protest groups which came into existence at various times in Western history and found themselves at variance with the dominant church. Landmark historians suggested that these groups held key convictions in common with the Baptists and for that reason constituted an unbroken succession of true Christianity from the first century into the present. However, other historians have been unable to document a continuous chain of direct influence from earlier to later groups. Likewise, the differences among the various sects generally cited and between them and the Baptists have been shown to be greater than the similarities. These factors have resulted in the waning of Landmark influence.

Currently, historians are divided between two basic theories of Baptist origins. One theory suggests that the movement finds its source in the continental Anabaptists of the sixteenth century, whereas the other understands Baptist beginnings solely in terms of the Puritan Reformation in England. Because "Anabaptist" was a term of derision used by the establishment throughout northern Europe and England to refer to all persons who rejected infant baptism, the early English sources are somewhat ambiguous. Since documentation of direct influence of continental Anabaptists on English Baptists is unavailable and since the Puritan background of the movement is undeniable, it is best to begin the story of the Baptists with Puritan England.

General Baptist Beginnings

Although the reformation spirit had been present within the established church in England at least from the days of John Wycliffe, the hopes of many to rid their church of what they saw as the evils of Catholicism and extend the Protestant Reformation to their land were kindled by King Henry VIII's break with Rome in 1534 and later by the coronation of the Protestant Queen Elizabeth I in 1558. But neither monarch was willing to inaugurate fully the program of the reformers. In response, a group of radical Protestants solidified by 1572. Because they desired to restore the English church to the purity of the apostolic era as found in the New Testament, they came to be called Puritans.

A highly significant area of disagreement between the Puritans and the English church was that of the proper form of church government. Although no one at first questioned the concept of a national church (i.e., that all citizens ought to belong to one established ecclesiastical structure and that dissenters ought to be persecuted), the Puritans objected to the episcopal system which the English church had inherited from Roman Catholicism. The radicals advocated the Presbyterian form of government, similar to that found in Calvin's Geneva, in which elected representatives, and not the bishops, formed the legislative body for the church.

Although some Puritans chose to remain in the Church of England and hope for a reformation from within, others, questioning the wisdom and validity of such a compromise, withdrew and formed underground congregations in which their ideals could be practiced. This experiment in covert congregations resulted in many of these Separatist Puritans rejecting Presbyterianism in favor of an even more radical ecclesiology, Congregationalism, which advocated the autonomy of the individual churches. Conflicts with the civil magistrates, which resulted from the Congregationalists' status as illegal dissenters, caused them to question the validity of government jurisdiction in religious affairs. Likewise, the personal commitment which membership in an underground church required resulted in a redefining of the church in terms of covenant—a people united together and to God by a mutual, voluntary covenant. A few of the more radical Separatists, having already judged the persecuting, nonreforming English church as a false church and "antichrist," came to question the validity of its sacraments as well.

In 1608, five years after the death of Elizabeth, a Separatist congregation led by John Smythe left Gainsborough, England, and resettled in Amsterdam, where another similar English church had already been established. As a result of his discussions with the Amsterdam church leaders, Smythe's Congregationalism took on a more radical tone. He came to deny that church elders had any authority whatsoever, even over the sacraments, except as delegated by the congregation. Similarly he suggested that the Separatists' condemnation of the English church demanded that they reject the baptism they had received at its hand. Finally, he understood the act of baptism as the public entrance into the covenant with God, a principle which he came to see as necessitating believer's baptism. Convinced by these considerations that no true church could be found anywhere and that he lived in a state of total apostasy, he decided to start anew. In 1609 Smythe dissolved the church of which he was pastor and embarked on an unheard of course of action, baptizing (by pouring) himself and his followers into a "true body," in order that the broken covenant might be correctly renewed. This bold act of Smythe is seen by many as the beginning of the modern Baptist movement.

In Holland Smythe also came into contact with the Mennonites. It is possible that their influence was instrumental in his rejection of Calvinist theology and his acceptance of another radical idea, religious liberty for all. In any case, these convictions were incorporated into the confession of faith adopted by his followers, who later returned to England under the leadership of Thomas Helwys. As the group members multiplied, they came to be known as General Baptists, because of their non-Calvinist emphasis on general atonement (Christ died for all, not merely for the elect).

Particular Baptist Beginnings

The beginning point of the General Baptists stands at the conclusion of a Separatist pathway. Another Baptist genesis, that of nonseparating Puritanism, resulted from a less radical route.

Although some Puritans, such as Smythe, concluded that separation from the established church was the best means to reformation, the majority disagreed and chose to remain in the English church. They did not find the national body to be totally apostate, as the Separatists did, but saw a kernel of the true church within the husk of corruption. Some nonseparating Puritans, however, did accept Congregationalism, and because they envisioned a national church consisting of a system of independent congregations, they were known as semi-Independents.

In 1616 a semi-Independent congregation was formed in London. This congregation later came to be called the Jacob-Lathrop-Jessey Church, after the names of its first pastors. During the next twenty-five years the congregation was racked with internal strife and external persecution. Finally in 1640 a group of church dissidents, who had come to reject infant baptism, sent one of their number, Richard Blunt, to Holland to receive immersion from the Mennonites. Upon his return the next year, he baptized the group's teacher, and then the two baptized fifty-one others. This event marked the beginning of a second Baptist group, the Particular Baptists. In contrast to Smythe's followers, they did not reject the Calvinist theology of the Puritans but held to the doctrine of particular or limited atonement (Christ died only for the elect).

Beginnings in New England

English Baptists trace their history to two unconnected events, Smythe's action in Amsterdam and the formation of Blunt's group in London. American Baptists find their genesis in Rhode Island in the legendary figure of Roger Williams. Williams arrived in the colony of Massachusetts at the time when the nonseparating Puritans of Boston were solidifying their hold on the colony at the expense of the Separatists who had arrived earlier at Plymouth. The Boston program included the establishment of Congregational churches consisting only of the elect, which were in turn supported by the civil magistrate. As soon as he arrived in Massachusetts, Williams questioned this program, based on his understanding of Calvinist theology. He denied that churches of the elect could be formed on earth, since the elect status of anyone was ultimately known only by God. Likewise, he claimed that the magistrate's task could not include the defense of the true faith, since faith, which comes solely by God's gift, cannot be forced on anyone by means of external coercion. This consideration caused Williams to limit the sphere of civil government to "the outer man" (i.e., public conduct) and to place "the inner man" (i.e., personal beliefs and convictions) beyond its reach.

Like many others, Williams began his pastoral career in the Church of England. But already in England he had become dissuaded first by the Puritans and then by the Separatists. After his arrival in the New World he was confronted with the same question that had plagued Smythe earlier: how could one retain the baptism of the English church after judging it to be apostate and after separating from it? His study of the New Testament solidified his rejection of that baptism, not just because it was performed by a false church, but also because it was performed on infants, in contrast to the believer's baptism of the early church. Soon thereafter his confrontation with Paul's stress on baptism as burial with Christ resulted in his acceptance of immersion as the proper mode.

Although it is possible that Williams came to an immersionist position somewhat soon after his arrival in New England, he did not act on these principles until he was banished from the Massachusetts colony. Once an exile in the wilderness of Rhode Island, however, the pioneer concluded that his circumstances demanded unusual action. In March, 1639, he was immersed by one of his followers, Ezekiel Holliman. Williams in turn baptized Holliman and about ten others, and the first immersionist church in the English-speaking world was formed.

These varying events in these different places were the beginnings of the modern Baptist movement. The genesis of the movement lies, at least in part, in the Congregational wing of the English Puritan party. On several occasions groups of believers were spawned for whom the basic convictions of the Congregationalists ultimately demanded the attempt to reestablish New Testament Christianity in a form which included believer's baptism. As the movement gained momentum, other congregations sprang up in old and New England and eventually throughout the world. Theological differences have emerged, just as there were theological differences at the beginning. Yet, these various churches and peoples find themselves bound together by a common desire to be the people of God according to Scripture and conscience, a desire which produces in them a loyalty to certain common convictions. Some of these are shared with other Christians; others are theirs alone. But when taken together these convictions, combined with a unique heritage and a unique history, mark these people as Baptists.

11

Baptist Emphases

In the past 380 years Baptists have grown to a community of global extent. They remain, however, a loosely organized group without international hierarchy, organizational unity, mandatory creed, or common liturgy. Likewise, they are diverse theologically, politically, ethnically, economically, and socially. Yet they remain loyal to certain general principles that have been emphasized by Baptists everywhere and at all times.

It is perhaps somewhat improper to call these principles "Baptist distinctives." Several of them have never been solely the property of Baptists, but rather belong to the Protestant heritage as a whole. Although early Baptists did stand alone in the defense of certain of these, their witness has resulted in an increased understanding and acceptance of such principles by many Christian traditions, especially in North America.

At the same time, however, there is something distinctively Baptist about the understanding of the Christian faith which places emphasis on this specific body of principles, for taken together they constitute an outlook which is unique within Christianity. Likewise, even those principles accepted from the common Protestant heritage have not been incorporated into the Baptist perspective unchanged. Rather, Baptists have sought to apply them in a manner which they perceive to be more consistent than that found in other traditions. Therefore, it is proper to enumerate a series of convictions which might be termed "Baptist emphases," in that together these principles constitute the unique Baptist contribution to Christianity.

Most of the principles that will be mentioned here have been discussed at greater length in preceding chapters. However, they will now be brought together in a more systematic fashion and in summary form. In all, seven convictions will come into focus, which together form an acrostic for the word BAPTIST:

Believer's baptism
Autonomy of the local congregation within the associational framework
Primacy of Scripture
True believers only in the church
Individual competency and believer priesthood
Separation of church and state
Two ordinances

The order in which these convictions are discussed will diverge from that of the acrostic. Two foundational principles will be treated initially, followed by a shorter capsulizing of five that may perhaps be understood as outgrowths of these.

Foundational Emphases
Primacy of Scripture

The self-conscious beginning point for the distinct emphasis of the Baptist tradition lies in a nonnegotiable commitment to the Bible as the primary source book for individual and corporate Christian life. From their early days as a persecuted sect Baptists have seen themselves as a people of and under the Book, as a people with an intense desire not only to study but also to live out the teachings of the Bible. This conviction was given classic formulation in 1833 in the first article of the New Hampshire Confession of faith:

> We believe the Holy Bible was written by men divinely inspired, and is a perfect treasure of heavenly instruction; that it has God for its author, salvation for its end, and truth, without any mixture of error, for its matter; that it reveals the principles by which God will judge us; and therefore is, and shall remain to the end of the world, the true centre of Christian union, and the supreme standard by which all human conduct, creeds, and opinions should be tried.

This foundational emphasis on the authority of Scripture is understandable when placed within the context of the question of authority raised by the Reformation. Although Christians have always acknowledged the Bible as authoritative, the exact role of the church as mediator of biblical authority has been problematic since the time of the early church. Perhaps the most elaborate response to this problem was developed by the Roman Catholic Church, which entrusted the task of proper biblical interpretation to the clergy and elevated church tradition to an authoritative status next to the Bible. According to this view, apostolic teaching is transmitted not only in the Bible but also through the tradition of the church. It was this understanding that allowed certain beliefs that are not explicitly taught in the Bible (such as the immaculate conception of Mary) to become part of the body of official church dogma. In the nineteenth century papal authority was also dogmatized. As a result the contemporary Roman Catholic Church accepts as infallible the doctrinal pronouncements which the pope makes when speaking as the vicar of Christ *(ex cathedra)*.

The developing Roman Catholic understanding was called into question by the Reformation. In that movement the twofold authority of Bible and tradition—the Bible as interpreted and augmented by church tradition—was set aside in favor of acceptance of the Bible as sole authority. Further, the people as a whole were seen as possessing the right to read and understand the Scriptures. Luther's commitment to this principle, *sola scriptura*, motivated his concern that the Bible be made available to all in the common language, rather than solely to the clergy in Latin.

Subsequent history has shown the difficulty of following this Reformation principle in a consistent manner. Some Christians give special status to the teachings of a church founder. Denominational creeds have also emerged, often claiming binding authority for denomination membership. Even local congregational tradition becomes endowed with implicit authority, as the argument "We've always done it this way" is seen as settling debated issues. Baptists, however, have sought to avoid these dangers and to hold to the Bible alone as the final authority.

Ultimately, primacy is given to Scripture because of its unique relationship to the Holy Spirit. In the past the Spirit was involved in the composition of the Bible by means of inspiration. Because God's Spirit was operative in the formation of Scripture (2 Peter 1:19-21), the documents themselves are "God-breathed" (2 Timothy 3:16-17). In the present the Spirit continues to be involved in the understanding and application of Scripture to each succeeding contemporary situation by means of illumination. The Spirit of Christ directs the Christian and the community by speaking through the pages of the Bible.

Baptists maintain that the Spirit speaking through the Bible must always be given preeminence in Christian life, although tradition, reason, and experience are not to be discounted. This emphasis on the sufficiency of Scripture is especially significant for the question of the use of church creeds. Although Baptists have repeatedly followed other groups in summarizing their convictions in "confessions of faith" for apologetic and instructive uses, these have been seen as valid and helpful only to the extent that they succinctly reflect scriptural teaching. Binding creeds have been consistently rejected as a usurpation of biblical authority and an infringement on individual competency. In short, Baptists have sought to stand consistently with Luther's position, as he purportedly outlined it for the Diet of Worms:

> Unless I am convinced by the testimony of Scripture or by evident reason— for I confide neither in the Pope or a council alone, since it is certain that they have erred and contradicted themselves—I am held fast by the Scripture adduced by me, and my conscience is taken captive by God's Word.[1]

Individual Competency and Believer Priesthood

The first foundational Baptist emphasis is concerned with religious authority. The second deals with the human person before God and declares that the individual is competent in religious affairs. As with the first, this conviction arose out of the conflicts of the Reformation. Medieval theology had developed an intricate system by means of which the grace of God could be received by sinful humanity. This system centered on the church as the dispenser of grace (sacramentarianism) and on a special class of people, the clergy, who acted on behalf of the church (sacerdotalism). Access to God, then, was seen as mediated by the clergy, who stood between God and the masses of adherents. The clergy acted on God's behalf dispensing God's grace and forgiveness to the people by means of the sacraments. The priests likewise acted on behalf of the laity by bringing their offerings to God through the mass and public prayers.

The Reformation challenged the concepts of mediated access and class priesthood. Instead, access to God was said to be direct: God's grace and forgiveness come directly to each believer, and each one may approach God directly through Christ and function in a priestly manner, offering one's prayers and oneself to God and interceding on behalf of others. In spite of these revolutionary ideas, the Reformers retained a high view of the church. They understood the true church as being marked by the orderly administration of the sacraments. This resulted in a retention of the emphasis on the clergy as those empowered to administer these rites and on the church as logically preceding the individual believer.

As the English Puritan movement progressed, a conscientious attempt was made by some in the Congregationalist wing to take the universal priesthood concept more seriously and consistently. These persons saw the church as a group of believers standing together in covenant with one

---

[1]Roland H. Bainton, *Here I Stand* (New York: Mentor Books, 1950), p. 144.

another and with God. This understanding in turn placed primary emphasis on the individual's standing before God, rather than on the church as a dispenser of grace. Religion was understood more in terms of personal conviction than reception of sacramental grace. Some also questioned the sole right of clergy to administer the sacraments, suggesting that this right lies in the congregation as a whole, which delegates the administration of the sacraments to congregationally selected leaders.

From their beginning Baptists championed these Congregationalist convictions. Smythe, Williams, and others agreed that religious belief is a matter of inner conviction, since the regenerating work of God's Spirit is experienced individually. This understanding came to be called "soul liberty" or "individual competency." Competency, however, does not suggest the presence of any innate ability of the individual to attain peace with God by personal effort. Rather, its intent is to protect God's sovereign activity in individual lives. God's call, it declares, is to the individual. And since faith entails existential commitment, only the individual can exercise faith. Each one, then, as an individual person must respond to God's call.

In a similar way competency seeks to underscore the individual as a responsible religious being in the sight of God. Each one must accept responsibility for all personal actions, since each will be judged individually by God. Of course, influences such as family, culture, and society affect decisions and actions. Yet ultimately all choices are made by individuals and therefore entail personal responsibility.

The principle of individual competency has certain implications for congregational life. Since each believer has received priestly privileges and responsibilities (believer priesthood), all members of the congregation are to participate in the corporate life. Specifically, worship is not an act done by the clergy for the people, but rather it is to be the corporate act of the gathered people led by the clergy as designated leaders. Similarly, congregational decision making is to be the prerogative of all, since each regenerate believer is competent to participate in the process of discerning the will of the Lord for the corporate community.

Resultant Emphases

Out of the interplay of these two foundational principles, primacy of Scripture and individual competency, arise five other significant convictions which belong to the Baptist heritage.

True Believers Only in the Church

Baptists followed their Congregationalist forebears in accepting the principle of regenerate church membership, or the pure church ideal, as it is sometimes called. This principle articulates a fundamental understanding concerning the nature of the church, namely, that it consists in a people standing in voluntary covenant with one another and God. This outlook suggests further that, as far as is possible, church membership, as participation in this covenant company, must be limited to those persons who are truly converted (true believers). Of course, the pure church ideal remains always an ideal. A pure congregation consisting only of regenerate members cannot be established by human beings, since no one can see the heart of another and thereby determine with certainty the status of the other before God.

The radical nature of the principle of regenerate church membership, however, comes into focus when it is put into the context of the various alternatives. In the era which saw the birth of the Baptist movement, the vast majority of church bodies advanced the principle of mixed church membership. The church was perceived by most Christians, whether Catholic or Protestant, as in some sense a dispenser of grace, a view in some ways reminiscent of the medieval understanding. Further, Protestants generally affirmed the concept of a national church, which maintained that the citizens of any nation ought to be members of the state-supported church. In such a situation, little concern was generally given to insure that all church members be regenerate.

In contrast to the mixed-membership practice of certain other bodies, Baptists have continually sought to take seriously the New Testament understanding of the church as the company of the redeemed. The teaching of the Scriptures, they maintain, is clear: church membership is to follow, not precede, personal faith and baptism (Acts 2:41). This scriptural principle is derived from individual competency as well, for if God's call to faith is issued to individuals, the church can be seen only as the company of believers (i.e., those who have responded to God's personal call).

Baptist commitment to the pure church ideal assumes concrete form in several ways. For example, church membership is extended only to those who express a personal desire to covenant together with the local body. Generally a testimony of personal conversion and baptism are required of all membership candidates. Similarly, church membership is never extended to infants or very young children, even if they are offspring of persons within the local congregation. In the same way, Baptists attempt to take seriously the New Testament concept of church discipline, which includes both the encouraging admonition of offenders and the severing of fellowship with unrepentant members. This final step is necessitated by the pure church ideal, since adamantly continuing in the practice of sin is a contradiction to one's verbal confession and an indication of an unregenerate status.

Autonomy and Association of the Congregations

This principle and the next two have been discussed at length in previous chapters. Local congregational autonomy declares that the lordship of Christ over his church is directly present in each local body apart from any mediating hierarchy external to it. Further, it suggests that the corporate community of believers in each location is competent to seek the will and mind of Christ for its own affairs. Hence, in addition to being a reflection of the New Testament pattern itself, congregational autonomy is an extension on the corporate level of the principle of individual competency and believer priesthood.

As has been pointed out previously, fidelity to the New Testament ecclesiological model demands that autonomy be balanced by a sense of corporate identity, which gives acknowledgment to the unity and interdependency of Christ's church everywhere. Their understanding of this has led most Baptist congregations to band together in voluntary associations of various types. By its voluntary nature an association upholds the autonomy of the member congregations. At the same time, as an expression of Christ's body on a broader scale, the association carries an advisory function which ought to be taken seriously by its constituency.

Two Ordinances

Traditionally Baptists have emphasized the ordained as opposed to the sacramentarian nature of the church's sacred observances. With the Reformed tradition they have accepted only two such practices, baptism and the Lord's Supper, as being truly ordained by the Lord of the church. Baptist rejection of sacramentarianism is an outworking of the primacy of Scripture and individual competency. This development must be understood in the context of the Reformation. Luther began the movement away from the medieval sacramental system by declaring that faith was necessary for the validity of any sacrament. Sacramentarianism, however, was not thereby totally eradicated. Many Protestants retained the belief that the acts themselves in some way mediate grace to the participant. The early Baptists, while not denying that the Holy Spirit utilizes the sacred practices, desired to shift the focus. For them these acts were vehicles for the expression of personal faith. In this way emphasis was placed upon the competent individual, who responds to God's personal call by obediently participating in observances which Christ himself commanded.

This view of the ordinances is in keeping with the Baptist understanding of the church as the regenerate people of God. The church is not the dispenser of grace to which one comes to receive salvation, but rather the corporate fellowship of the redeemed. Its sacred practices, therefore, are not the means by which saving grace is received. Rather, these acts are public testimonies and celebrations of God's gracious provision of salvation granted to his people. As such, their observance strengthens the participant in one's personal walk as a believer.

Believer's Baptism

Many suggest that believer's baptism or even the mode of immersion is the chief hallmark of the Baptist tradition. Actually, however, this significant emphasis is a logical outworking of other more basic Baptist convictions. On the one hand, Baptists claim that New Testament teaching itself demands believer's baptism. The texts which support this conviction need not be repeated here. On the other hand, Baptists reject infant baptism in favor of believer's baptism, not only because of their understanding of the New Testament precedence, but also because this practice is more consistent with their understanding of individual competency, the nature of the church, and the significance of the ordinances. God's call, they maintain, is directed to the individual, who in turn is to respond with repentance and faith. The believer's response is expressed publicly in baptism. This ordinance therefore, is seen by Baptists as the God-given vehicle for the public declaration of inward, personal faith, and not as a rite which creates that faith, as maintained by certain other traditions. Infant baptism, in turn, is defective for it cannot function as the personal public testimony that the gospel ordinance is designed to be.

Beginning with Luther, Protestants sought to maintain infant baptism, while acknowledging the necessity of faith for a proper sacrament. Some, following Luther, speak of "infant faith," which obviously must be quite different from the conscious faith which Baptists find in the New Testament. Some Reformed church bodies look instead to the parents, sponsors, or corporate community to confess the faith which the infant will one day be able to acknowledge. Baptists find this to be incompatible with the principle of regenerate church membership. Thus, the desire for consistency is a significant motivation behind the Baptist emphasis on believer's baptism.

Separation of Church and State

Although the Reformation challenged many aspects of medieval theology, it retained the close tie which had existed between the civil government and the church since Constantine and maintained the national church ideal (i.e., the suggestion that all citizens should be members of the established church). In sixteenth-century Germany this principle found expression in the territorial system, in which each prince had the right to determine which church would receive official status in the province of his jurisdiction. Even many of the Puritan reformers in both old and New England envisioned a Christian state with the civil magistrate as the defender of the true faith.

As a dissenting minority, Baptists were subjected to ecclesiastical and civil persecution in both Puritan commonwealths.

In contrast to many continental and English reformers, the early Baptists came to advocate toleration of religious dissent and even a new understanding of the relationship between the civil and ecclesiastical spheres. Lying behind the political reform which they advocated was a commitment to religious liberty for all. This view upholds the right of each individual to determine personal religious convictions or to be without convictions, apart from any civil coercion or hindrance. Religious liberty also includes the right to practice and propagate one's convictions within the protection of the law, as far as one's actions do not cause injury to another.

The political order in which religious liberty is practiced came to be known as separation of church and state. This principle places restrictions on both spheres. Separation denies the civil government the prerogative of using compulsion in matters of the religious beliefs of its citizens (unless genuine injury to others results from the exercise of such beliefs). Further, no government has the right to meddle in the internal affairs of the church or determine the nature of the church's message. Likewise, no religious prerequisites for public office or voting are to be devised. For the church, separation debars any direct meddling by an ecclesiastical body in governmental affairs. Likewise, the civil power may not be used as a means to dictate to the nation as a whole any purely sectarian policy.

Separation of church and state has been misunderstood in recent years. It is neither intended to eliminate religion from national life nor to silence the church's voice in matters of civil concern. On the contrary, churches are always to be free to function in a prophetic manner, speaking out concerning the moral issues which confront nation and world. Separation seeks only to prohibit the civil government from employing its authority to advance the cause of one religious body at the expense of others or to advance the cause of religion at the expense of the nonreligious. Similarly, separation is intended to allow religious groups to carry on their own distinctive activities apart from the fear of persecution or reprisal.

The Baptist emphasis on religious liberty and separation of church and state may also be understood as a consistent outworking of other fundamental principles. Their reading of the New Testament causes Baptists to see religion fundamentally in terms of the status of the individual before God. Thus, Christian faith begins with the individual heart and heartfelt inner convictions. If this is the case, then true religion simply cannot be advanced by means of external coercion of any form. Faith is the product of hearing the gospel message, becoming convinced of its validity and responding to it. Therefore, Christian truth is best served by a climate in which it is free to do its own convincing work.

The Baptist understanding of the nature of the church is another factor which results in an emphasis on separation of church and state. Only those who respond freely to God's call with inner conviction are proper members of the true church. As the voluntary society of the redeemed, the covenant community can never be coterminous with any political boundary. No civil government, then, has the right to coerce its citizens to become a part of any ecclesiastical body. In fact, the cause of the church is best served when the church is left free to carry on its task of gospel proclamation and when the hearers of the gospel are left free to be convinced of Christian truth by the gospel's own power.

Religious liberty has not always been a popular cause. Baptists who have become part of the religious establishment understand the temptations which such status entails. Yet, whenever they are true to their heritage, Baptists champion the cause of liberty for all. This was eloquently articulated by the Baptist George W. Truett in 1920:

> Baptists have one consistent record concerning liberty throughout all their long and eventful history. They have never been a party to oppression of conscience. They have forever been the unwavering champions of liberty, both religious and civil. Their contention now is, and has been, and please God, must ever be, that it is the natural and fundamental and indefensible right of every human being to worship God or not, according to the dictates of his conscience, and, as long as he does not infringe upon the right of others, he is to be held accountable alone to God for all religious beliefs and practices. Our contention is not for mere toleration, but for absolute liberty. There is a wide difference between toleration and liberty. Toleration implies that somebody falsely claims the right to tolerate. Toleration is a concession, while liberty is a right. Toleration is a matter of expediency, while liberty is a matter of principle. Toleration is a gift from man, while liberty is a free gift from God. It is the consistent and insistent contention of our Baptist people, always and everywhere, that religion must be forever voluntary and uncoerced, and that it is not the prerogative of any power, whether civil or ecclesiastical, to compel men to conform to any religious creed or form of worship, or to pay taxes for the support of a religious organization to which they do not belong and in whose creed they do not believe. God wants free worshipers and no other kind.[2]

[2] George W. Truett, "Baptists and Religious Liberty," *God's Call to America* (New York: George H. Doran, Co., 1924), pp. 32-33.

12 The Baptist Movement Today

In the four centuries since John Smythe boldly baptized himself and his followers and thereby constituted the first modern Bapist congregation, the Baptist movement has grown and spread throughout the world. Today Baptists are present in more than 148 countries, comprising the second most widespread Christian faith group. Individual churches number more than 140,000 with an additional 36,000 preaching/mission stations. These churches include some 33.7 million members, with the wider fellowship numbering close to 47 million. The great majority are found in the United States. But sizable numbers are also present in India, the Soviet Union, Brazil, Burma, the United Kingdom, Zaire, Canada, Romania, and Nigeria.

Although all Baptist churches are self-governing, most congregations cooperate with others locally, regionally, nationally, and internationally. About 87 percent of all Baptists are associated through national conventions with the Baptist World Alliance (BWA), which consists of more than 110 Baptist bodies. The BWA was formed in 1905, when 3,000 Baptists from 23 nations met in London, England. The purpose of this voluntary organization is spelled out in its constitution as revised at the Fourteenth Congress in Toronto, 1980:

Preamble

The Baptist World Alliance, extending over every part of the world, exists as an expression of the essential oneness of Baptist people in the Lord Jesus Christ, to impart inspiration to the fellowship, and to provide channels for sharing concerns and skills in witness and ministry. This Alliance recognizes the traditional autonomy and independence of churches and general bodies.

Objectives

Under the guidance of the Holy Spirit, the objectives of the Baptist World Alliance shall be to:

1. Promote Christian fellowship and cooperation among Baptists throughout the world.
2. Bear witness to the gospel of Jesus Christ and assist unions and conventions in their divine task of bringing all people to God through Jesus Christ as Savior and Lord.
3. Promote understanding and cooperation among Baptist bodies and with other Christian groups, in keeping with our unity in Christ.
4. Act as an agency for the expression of biblical faith and historically distinctive Baptist principles and practices.
5. Act as an agency of reconciliation seeking peace for all persons, and uphold the claims of fundamental human rights, including full religious liberty.
6. Serve as a channel for expressing Christian social concern and alleviating human need.
7. Serve in cooperation with member bodies as a resource for the development of plans for evangelism, education, church growth, and other forms of mission.
8. Provide channels of communication dealing with work related to these objectives through all possible media.

The BWA exists to assist its member bodies in fulfilling their common tasks. As such it serves as an encouraging reminder of the worldwide Christian community. Throughout its history the organization has been active in various programs, including education, evangelism, inter-church fellowship, and study commissions. World congresses are held every five years, as are world youth conferences.

One significant program which has received much attention is BWA involvement in religious liberty issues worldwide. These joint international efforts have resulted in certain definite successes, including the legal importation of Bibles and religious literature into eastern European countries and the release of several dissident religious leaders.

Perhaps the most well-known area of BWA involvement is relief. The devastation of World War I evoked a major Baptist relief project. Then in 1943 in the midst of the destruction of the Second World War, the BWA executive committee created the Committee on World Emergency Relief, launching the present program. What began as an attempt to meet needs in war-devastated central Europe has in the intervening decades expanded in size, extent, and commitment. Projects are under way in more than 40 countries, representing every continent, at a cost of $1.2 million. Relief programs include not only necessities, such as food, clothing, shelter, and medicine, but also Bibles, hospitals, and church buildings, irrigation and well-digging projects, and vocational schools. A unique feature of BWA relief is that whenever possible aid is channeled through local Baptist bodies, thereby eliminating the high administrative costs of many interdenominational programs.

In the early 1960s a regional body functioning within the BWA was formed, called the North American Baptist Fellowship (N.A.B.F.). Currently seven of the eleven BWA members in the United States plus the Baptist Federation of Canada and the National Baptist Convention of Mexico are banded together in this voluntary organization (United States members are: American Baptist Churches in the U.S.A., General Association of General Baptists, National Baptist Convention of America, North American Baptist Conference, Progressive National Baptist Convention, Seventh Day Baptist General Conference, Southern Baptist Convention). As its name and affiliation suggest, the N.A.B.F. seeks to promote cooperation among Baptists and to further BWA objectives on the North American continent. To this end representatives of member bodies gather yearly to exchange ideas. In addition, consultations for denominational leaders are held and Baptist cooperation on the local level is encouraged.

Another significant cooperative venture in the United States is the Baptist Joint Committee on Public Affairs (BJC), which stands at the forefront in articulating to the national government Baptist concerns on issues of religious liberty. This committee consists of pastors, denominational leaders, and laypersons who represent nine Baptist fellowships in North America (American Baptist Churches in the U.S.A., Baptist General Conference, National Baptist Convention of America, National Baptist Convention, Inc., North American Baptist Conference, Progressive National Baptist Convention, Seventh Day Baptist General Conference, Southern Baptist Convention, and the Baptist Federation of Canada).

The genesis of the BJC is found in a group of Baptists of various backgrounds who began meeting in the nation's capital in the late 1930s, in order to monitor world events affecting religious liberty. The committee structure was formalized in 1946, with the financial support of the American and Southern Baptist conventions. Joseph M. Dawson of the Southern Baptist Convention (SBC) was called to become the first executive director of the new committee. This position has been subsequently filled by C. Emanuel Carlson, Baptist General Conference (BGC); James E. Wood (SBC); and James M. Dunn (SBC).

Since its founding the BJC has dealt mainly with public policy issues which center on church-state relations. Its primary mandate is to monitor government actions which involve intrusion of the state into church affairs.

In fulfilling this task the committee seeks to act in two directions. On the one hand, it articulates Baptist concerns to the national government. Naturally, Baptists may from time to time differ among themselves concerning contemporary issues, and therefore the BJC cannot attempt to speak the mind of all individuals. Its purpose is rather that of safeguarding the interests of its constituency by voicing Baptist religious liberty concerns in view of pending governmental decisions or current situations. On the other hand, the committee informs its member bodies concerning those governmental actions which affect church-state relations and the religious life of the nation.

To assist the committee, a staff office is maintained in Washington, D.C., which can more readily monitor governmental activities and inform government decision-making bodies of committee concerns. Several basic programs are maintained by the committee and its staff as part of their overall task. The government relations program is designed to provide a prophetic Baptist voice to federal agencies. A second program, information services, seeks to assist the BJC constituency in keeping abreast of current developments in national life. The public affairs study and research program analyzes government decisions and regulations, especially for their significance for religious liberty. Finally, through the program of correlation of Baptist influence, the BJC seeks to advise constituent denominations concerning appropriate actions in areas of public affairs. In this way the various Baptist bodies are assisted in speaking to crucial issues concerning church-state relations with one voice and in a manner consistent with Baptist tradition.

Of the 33.7 million Baptists worldwide, 29 million or about 85 percent are found in the United States with an additional 200,000 in Canada. Baptists in America are a pluralistic group theologically, economically, ethnically, and politically. This pluralism, historical factors, and differences in certain aspects of polity have resulted in the formation of many independent associational bodies. In the United States well over two dozen different conferences or associational groups currently exist. By far the largest body is the nearly 14 million member Southern Baptist Convention (SBC), which was formed in 1845. Although originally localized in the Confederate States, the SBC has spread throughout the nation during the twentieth century. Next in size are three predominantly black conventions, which together number about 10 million. The American Baptist Churches in the U.S.A. (formerly the Northern Baptist Convention) represents about 1.6 million Baptists. In addition to these, five smaller groups, ranging in size from just over 500 to nearly 140,000 participate in the BWA. Some Baptist churches have chosen not to affiliate with any association, although many of these do maintain informal fellowship ties with similarly inclined congregations. Baptists in the United States, numbering about 29 million, comprise a significant percentage of the total population. In Canada the situation is somewhat different; the 200,000 Canadian Baptists account for only 3.5 percent of the national population. In spite of their relatively small numerical strength, Canadian Baptists are a significant member of the national religious community and carry on a vigorous work in all sections of the nation.

Baptists in Canada are divided into several independent fellowships. At least four Canadian bodies are linked organizationally with groups in the United States. Of these, the North American Baptist Conference and the Baptist General Conference include Canadian constituencies which are relatively large. The Canadian Baptist Conference, found in Alberta and British Columbia, is an offshoot of the Southern Baptist Convention. A fourth group, the Atlantic Association of Free Will Baptists, is quite small. The most prominent strictly Canadian bodies are the Fellowship of Evangelical Baptist Churches in Canada and the Baptist Federation of Canada. The 125,000-member federation is by far the largest Baptist denomination in the nation.

Baptist influence on American life has been great. The freedom and individualism stressed throughout United States history has produced a climate which has fostered unparalleled growth of Baptist churches in this land, so that this group now comprises the largest American Protestant body. Baptists in turn have been in a position to encourage the advancement of certain of their fundamental concerns in the nation as a whole. Most notable is the universal practice of voluntary church support in America, which forms a stark contrast to the long history of religious taxation in Europe. Prior to the American Revolution, Baptists stood nearly alone in the struggle to disestablish privileged religious bodies. But since that time, many American churches have found themselves deeply influenced by Baptist ecclesiology. In fact, in the twentieth century the struggle to maintain religious liberty, which was originally a Baptist hallmark, has been joined by adherents of many church bodies whose heritage lies in state support and religious intolerance. Unfortunately, however, there are some Baptists who have forgotten the sacrifices of their forebears and are in danger of being lulled into the establishmentarian mind-set which has been gaining ground throughout North America in recent years. The Baptist vision of the faith must be reaffirmed anew by each succeeding generation, if the denomination is to continue to make its contribution to the church of Christ.

13 ✤ Baptist Bodies in America

The associational principle—autonomous congregations linked together in an association framework—is a significant aspect of Baptist polity. In America, associations developed quite early. The first was formed in 1670 by four Rhode Island churches. The Philadelphia Baptist Association, founded in 1707, became a significant force in the subsequent growth of the denomination throughout the colonies. Associations were also established in Massachusetts, North Carolina, Virginia, and Nova Scotia (Canada) during the eighteenth century.

Although kinship beyond associational ties flourished in the colonial era, the first organizational expression of a national Baptist consciousness came in 1814. In that year a convention of associations was convened; it was called "the General Missionary Convention of the Baptist Denomination in the United States of America for Foreign Missions." As similar meetings came to be held every three years, "Triennal Convention" became the generally used designation. Other cooperative efforts were launched, including the American Baptist Publication Society (1824) and the American Baptist Home Missionary Society (1832). These various programs were organized as independent agencies, all of which appealed to the Baptist constituency for support.

The Baptists in the 1820s comprised a group of loosely joined associations and state conventions which cooperated in enterprises of common concern. This voluntary approach which characterized Baptist life from its inception is one significant factor lying behind the presence today of a multitude of independent Baptist fellowships in the United States. (Various lists include as many as fifty-two groups.) Some of these are largely regional, the product of associations which were never a part of wider cooperative activities. Others are the result of differences in outlook which developed among members of a larger body. Fellowships in a third group originally were ethnic in orientation.

In the twentieth century several Baptist fellowships have banded together in various cooperative organizations, including the Baptist World Alliance (BWA). In this chapter, the BWA members in the United States will be highlighted. Then several other representative American groups will be mentioned, followed by a sketch of Baptists in Canada.

American Baptist Churches in the United States

The fellowship which may claim continuous organizational history from the Triennial Convention is known today as the American Baptist Churches in the U.S.A. (ABC, USA). The first half of the nineteenth century was a period of rapid expansion for Baptists in America. By 1843 twenty-five state conventions were in existence, twenty of which were related to the American Baptist Home Mission Society. However, in 1845 a separate Southern Baptist Convention was formed, partly due to the slavery issue and partly because the Southern constituency favored a more centralized structure. The northern Baptists continued the societal system, with the various organizations holding annual meetings simultaneously.

Following the Civil War expansion in the North and West continued. New educational institutions were founded, as were women's missionary societies and various benevolent agencies. To alleviate confusion and competition among the Baptist enterprises and as "an organized expression of denomination unity," the Northern Baptist Convention was created in 1907. The various societies, missions, publications became cooperating societies; the state conventions became affiliating organizations; and the local churches became the basis of representation at convention meetings. The denominational name was changed in 1950 to the American Baptist Convention. The current name was adopted in 1972. Difficulties inherent in combining the system of local church representation with the society organizational method have necessitated various structural changes since 1907. This restructuring has produced a fuller integration of the various cooperating agencies in the ABC, USA.

The American Baptist fellowship has witnessed repeated internal dissension, especially in the twentieth century. Theological inclusiveness resulted in the withdrawal of conservative factions on several occasions. Yet, this open theological stance also allowed the merger of the Free Will (1911),

Norwegian (1956), and Danish Baptists (1958) with the ABC, USA. The American Baptist Churches are perhaps the most ecumenically oriented of the Baptist family in America. This orientation is rooted in the interdenominational activities, comity arrangements, and open Communion stance which characterized Northern Baptists in the nineteenth century. The ABC, USA is a member body in the National Council and the World Council of Churches and carries on ecumenical dialogues with various groups.

American Baptists have always been a missionary-minded people. In fact, one impetus for the founding of the Triennial Convention was the desire to provide support for the work of Adoniram Judson and Luther Rice in Asia. Home missions and missions to immigrants were also at the forefront of American Baptist work in the nineteenth century. The foreign mission emphasis continues today through direct support of Baptist work in several countries and through cooperation with the BWA.

At present more than 5,800 churches in thirty-seven region/state/city conventions or associations are affiliated in the national body. Total membership exceeds 1.6 million. Denominational offices are located in Valley Forge, Pennsylvania.

Southern Baptist Convention

Baptist work in the South, begun in the seventeenth century, had already outpaced the work in the North before the rift occurred in 1845. The founding of a separate Southern convention was precipitated by a crisis in 1844 centering on the refusal by the American Baptist Home Mission Society to appoint a slaveholder as a missionary. The next year the Society expressed the desirability of separate Northern and Southern home missions organizations. A meeting of Baptists in the South was held one month later, May, 1845, and the Southern Baptist Convention (SBC) was born.

The new convention departed from the society model favored in the North. It was structured as a single organization, and in the words of its first president was "one Convention, embodying the whole Denomination, with separate and distinct Boards, for each object of benevolent enterprise." By 1860 four new state conventions had been added to the original nine, so that the SBC spanned all the southern and border states.

Home mission work was hampered by the Civil War. After the war the convention voted against reunion with the northern societies, and a trend toward increased independent activity by the SBC developed in the following decades. Eventually even a Southern Baptist publication enterprise was launched, which was placed under the auspices of the Sunday School Board in 1891. Home mission work was expanded into the Southwest and to Indians and blacks. In the 1850s the first SBC missionaries were sent to

China. The foreign mission thrust was greatly expanded in various continents during the last half of the century.

Since World War II Southern Baptist churches have been established beyond the original geographical base in the South. Today the work is found in all fifty states and has even spilled over into the western Canadian provinces. Phenomenal growth has made the convention, now numbering more than 14 million people, the largest Protestant body in America. More than 36,000 churches are organized into 1,196 associations and 34 state conventions.

Until recently, the convention was largely untouched by internal ferment as Southern Baptists tended to be intensely evangelistic and mildly Calvinistic. However, the cohesion and theological consensus which has characterized the convention in the past is currently undergoing strain.

The Southern Baptist Convention has largely been uninvolved in ecumenical enterprises. It has, however, assumed its position in Baptist circles as the largest Baptist fellowship. The SBC plays a significant role in various inter-Baptist organizations, providing both leadership and financial resources. The convention offices and many of the eleven boards and commissions are located in Nashville, Tennessee.

National Baptist Convention

Although black presence and involvement in Baptist work dates much earlier, the first black congregation was established by slaves in Silver Bluff, South Carolina, sometime before 1775. Thereafter the work developed rapidly throughout the South. In the North, black churches emerged after 1800, the first ones in Boston, New York, and Philadelphia.

Foreign mission work began in 1821, when Lott Carey and Collins Teague were sent to Liberia by the Triennial Convention. Home missions expanded into the Midwest, resulting in the founding of the first black association in Ohio in 1836. Forty-three years later the vision of a black missionary to Africa, W. W. Colley, resulted in the formation of the Foreign Mission Baptist Convention of the U.S.A. Two other national organizations followed: a coordinating body called the American National Baptist Convention (1886) and the Baptist National Education Convention (1893). The three merged in 1895 to form the National Baptist Convention.

One year later the convention home mission board established the National Baptist Publishing Board. This enterprise became the focal point of controversy, which resulted in an organizational division in the convention in 1915. One faction sought to bring the publication agency under convention control by means of incorporation. A convention charter was developed, but the publication board could not be compelled to come under the convention umbrella. The opposing faction, which supported the secretary of the publication board, reorganized without incorporation as the National Baptist Convention of America.

Another controversy resulted in the formation of a third convention in 1961. The issue was the growing discontent within the National Baptist Convention, Inc. concerning certain organizational matters, including the length of tenure of the convention president. A meeting of those who supported the four-year tenure rule adopted in 1952 was held in Cincinnati, Ohio. Out of this meeting arose the Progressive National Baptist Convention, Inc.

The largest of the three bodies is the National Baptist Convention, U.S.A., Inc., with 6.3 million members in 27,000 congregations. The National Baptist Convention of America has a membership of 3.5 million in 12,400 churches. Membership in the Progressive National Baptist Convention has grown to 700,000 in 1,534 churches. All three bodies are engaged in missionary activities, cooperate with the BWA, and hold membership in the National Council and the World Council of Churches.

In addition to the three National Baptist Conventions there are several smaller black Baptist groups. Black churches are also found in other fellowships, especially among the American Baptist Churches. Likewise, individual blacks hold membership in congregations of many Baptist bodies.

Smaller Fellowships in the BWA

In addition to the five larger bodies mentioned thus far, six other Baptist groups in the United States are members of the BWA. Two bodies will be mentioned only in passing. The Lott Carey Baptist Foreign Mission Convention is an early offshoot of the National Baptist Convention. Apparently all its member congregations are now affiliated with other BWA member conventions. The Union of Latvian Baptists in America is a very small group, numbering 563 members in eight congregations.

Baptist General Conference

The Baptist General Conference (BGC) began as a mission work among Swedish immigrants to North America. Gustaf Palmquist came to Illinois in 1851 as the spiritual leader of a group of Swedish Lutheran pietists. In 1852 he was baptized and ordained a Baptist minister. Later that year he formed a Swedish Baptist congregation in Rock Island, Illinois. Other churches were organized during the next decade, and a missionary fellowship for the Swedish work was formed with the support of the Northern Baptists. A theological seminary and a denominational paper were founded in 1871. In 1879 a national conference, the Swedish Baptist General Conference of America, was formed. Foreign mission work began in 1888 in cooperation with the American Baptist Foreign Mission Society.

A transition to the English language was initiated after World War I, followed by a change in the conference name in 1945. BGC missionary support, separate from the American Baptists since 1944, is channeled to eight nations. Rapid growth in recent years has brought the conference membership to 128,000 in 715 churches in the U.S.A. and 5,600 in 68 churches in Canada. The conference office is located near Chicago, Illinois.

General Association of General Baptists

John Smythe and Thomas Helwys followed the Arminian doctrine of a general atonement, that is, that Jesus died for all and not merely for the elect. Although many New England Baptists adhered to this position, they were overwhelmed by the Calvinist Baptists during the eighteenth century. The General Association of General Baptists was organized in 1870, following the establishment of Arminian churches in the Midwest beginning in 1823.

In addition to Arminian doctrine General Baptists are characterized by associational presbyteries consisting of area ordained clergy. These bodies examine candidates for ministry and deacon service. Foreign mission work of this group is supported in four countries. General Baptist membership numbers 75,000 in 870 churches. The denominational office is in Poplar Bluff, Missouri.

North American Baptist Conference

The North American Baptist (N.A.B.) Conference history resembles that of the BGC, having begun as a mission work among German immigrants. Although German-speaking churches were established in various locations at about the same time, the Philadelphia church started by Konrad Anton Fleischmann in 1843 is considered the oldest. These scattered churches resulted in the formation first of two and subsequently of nine regional conferences. The first general conference met in 1865; it was the forebear of the current triennial meeting.

A theological school was begun as part of Rochester Divinity School in 1865, supported heavily, as was the work in general, by the Northern Baptists.

Steps toward a language transition were inaugurated early in the twentieth century, but German immigration after each world war underscored the need for the ministry of German-speaking churches. Currently, however, nearly all churches use English exclusively.

Foreign mission work is supported in Cameroon, Nigeria, Japan, and Brazil. Membership totals about 60,000 in more than 350 churches, of which more than 100 churches with a membership of over 16,000 are located in Canada. The conference office is near Chicago.

Seventh Day Baptist General Conference

Seventh Day Baptists were present in England at least as early as 1617. The first congregation in America was founded in 1671, when a dispute over the sabbath question developed in the Newport, Rhode Island, Baptist Church after the arrival of Rev. Stephen Mumford, a London Seventh Day Baptist. During the next thirty years churches were established in Philadelphia and Piscataway, New Jersey; these churches were nurtured in part by immigration from England. From these three congregations the work spread slowly throughout the colonies and west to the frontier.

The Seventh Day Baptist General Conference was founded in 1801 to assist in organizing home and foreign missions. Today membership is more than 5,000 in 63 congregations. In 1965 the Seventh Day Baptist World Federation was formed which includes denominations in thirteen nations on four continents.

The chief difference between the Seventh Day Baptists and the others is their conviction that the God-ordained day for corporate worship is the seventh day, Saturday. The conference office is in Plainfield, New Jersey.

Other Baptist Fellowships in the United States

Although the large majority of Baptists in America are bonded together through the BWA and the North American Baptist Fellowship, there are significant numbers who have not joined these intra-Baptist organizations. A few Baptist congregations are totally independent. Most, however, co-operate with associations. For various doctrinal or organizational reasons some associations do not see fellowship with the wider Baptist family as either necessary or possible.

Already at the founding of the Triennial Convention certain Baptists objected to the organizing of a society beyond the local congregation which would solicit funds and oversee missions activity. One early center of opposition was the Kehukee Association of North Carolina, but by 1840 negative reaction had spread to the mid-Atlantic region and to the West. Those who opposed the "innovations" developed a consciousness of being the "true" or "primitive Baptists." Separate associations emerged, which were solely advisory in nature, allowing the local congregations to remain totally autonomous. With the exception of the predominantly black National Primitive Baptist Convention of the U.S.A., organized in 1907, no strong national denomination developed among the various Primitive Baptist associations. Estimates place their numbers at 72,000 in 1,000 congregations.

Old Landmarkism, a nineteenth-century movement which gained considerable strength especially in the South, centered on the question concerning the true church. A succession of "true churches" from the New Testament to the present was outlined. All non-Baptist congregations were rejected as false churches. Baptism by any other church, called alien baptism, was rejected, as was non-Baptist ordination. Closed Communion was likewise practiced. Landmarkism remained unorganized until the end of the century. Since 1899, however, several denominations have been formed, including the American Baptist Association (ABA) (founded in 1905) with a current membership of about 225,000 in more than 1,600 churches, and the Baptist Missionary Association of America, the product of a controversy in the ABA in 1949, now numbering more than 228,000 in nearly 1,400 churches.

In the first half of the twentieth century the Northern Baptist Convention (NBC) was infected by the fundamentalist-modernist controversy. Points at issue were doctrinal, ethical, and organizational. Conservatives tended to fear the growing centralization signaled by the formation of the convention, while demanding that the Foreign Mission Society support only those missionaries who held to a strong conservative Baptist position. In 1920 the Fundamentalist Fellowship was formed within the convention. After an unsuccessful attempt to win adoption by the NBC of the New Hampshire Confession of Faith, part of the conservative faction formed the Baptist Bible Union in 1922, which ten years later gave way to the General Association of Regular Baptists. This body, which is doctrinally separatist, fundamentalist, and premillennial, numbers more than 300,000 in nearly 1,600 congregations.

The conservatives who remained within the NBC focused their support on the Conservative Baptist Foreign Mission Society (CBFMS), established in 1943. The problem which this ignited in the convention resulted in the formation of the Conservative Baptist Association (CBA) in 1946, which gradually separated from the NBC. The CBA retained the society structure of the nineteenth century, becoming largely a doctrine-based fellowship for congregations supporting the CBFMS and its home missions counterpart. Although internal controversy in the 1950s resulted in further splintering within the movement, the CBA continued to grow and currently numbers about 225,000 in more than 1,100 congregations. Association offices are located in Wheaton, Illinois.

Baptists in Canada

Baptist history in Canada begins in the eighteenth century with the efforts of missionaries from New England. A congregation was organized in Horton (now Wolfville), Nova Scotia, in 1763. Following the Revolutionary War an influx of American loyalists to eastern Canada strengthened the Baptist work in the region. In the nineteenth century further growth was sparked by Baptist immigrants from Scotland, England, and French-speaking Switzerland. The activities of the Underground Railroad prior to the American

Civil War resulted in the formation of black congregations. Later in the century the westward migration brought Baptists to the prairie provinces and British Columbia.

Baptist Federation of Canada

Beyond the various local associations, three major regional conventions developed: the Baptist Union of Ontario and Quebec, originally founded in 1880; the Convention of Atlantic Baptists, which was the result of the merger of the Free Baptists (Arminian) and the Regular Baptists (Calvinist) in 1906; and the Baptist Union of Western Canada, established in 1909. These regional bodies formed the Baptist Federation of Canada in 1944, which was later joined by the French-speaking union established earlier. The Federation membership now stands at nearly 132,000 in 1,100 congregations.

The Fellowship of Evangelical Baptist Churches in Canada

At the close of the First World War the fundamentalist-modernist controversy caused division in the Ontario-Quebec convention. In 1927 the conservatives established the Union of Regular Baptist Churches, which itself was hampered by internal disputes during the next twenty-two years. From it the Fellowship emerged in 1953. In the meantime associations of theologically conservative Baptists had been formed in British Columbia (1927) and Alberta (1930). These joined the Fellowship in the 1960s. Currently the national body numbers about 54,000 members in more than 400 congregations.

Other Baptist Bodies

In addition to the Federation and the Fellowship, Canadian Baptists are organized into several smaller denominations. Some of these originated as ethnic-oriented fellowships among German (North American Baptist Conference), Swedish (Baptist General Conference), Ukrainian, and Slavic peoples. Other groups arose out of doctrinal disputes within a larger body (e.g., the Association of Regular Baptist Churches and the Fellowship of Fundamental Baptist Churches). There are also two Primitive Baptist bodies. One additional association, the Canadian Baptist Conference, is the product of recent Southern Baptist work in the western provinces. Of these smaller groups, the North American Baptists, who are closely affiliated with their U.S. counterpart, are by far the most numerous, numbering nearly 17,000 in more than 100 churches.

Appendixes

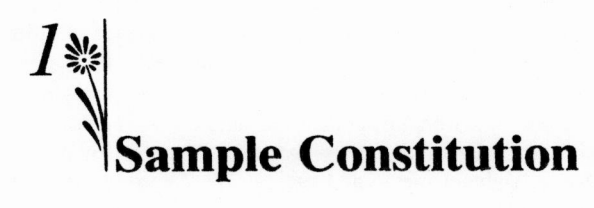

Sample Constitution

The following Constitution is an example of how the congregational structure outlined in this book might take shape in a local setting. The basic format has been adapted from the documents of the Southdale Community Baptist Church, Winnipeg, Manitoba.

A. NAME

This organization shall be known as _____ Baptist Church of _____ .

B. PURPOSE

Our main purpose for existing is to glorify God. We believe this will happen as we maintain a balanced ministry of corporate worship, mutual edification (educating and nurturing the congregational membership), and outreach (evangelizing and making disciples of others; serving the world in the name of Jesus Christ), as the following Constitution and Bylaws may determine.

C. STATEMENT OF FAITH

1. We believe in the one true God, the Creator and Redeemer, eternally existent and known to us in three Persons.
2. We believe in the Lord Jesus Christ, divine and human, who suffered a vicarious and atoning death, rose from the dead and will return in power.

3. We believe in the Holy Spirit who regenerates sinful humanity through repentance and faith in Jesus Christ and by whose indwelling the Christian is enabled to live a godly life.
4. We believe the Bible to be the inspired, infallible, authoritative Word of God for matters of faith and practice.
5. We believe in the spiritual unity of all believers in the Church of our Lord Jesus Christ.
6. We believe that each believer will be resurrected to eternal life, whereas the unrighteous will be raised to judgment.

D. *CHURCH COVENANT*

Having been led by the Spirit of God to receive Jesus the Christ as our Lord and Savior, and having given public confession of our faith through baptism in the name of the triune God, we do now in the presence of God joyfully and sincerely enter into covenant with one another as one body in Christ.

We determine as a body of believers that our primary purpose is to bring glory to God through worship, edification, and outreach. We determine to walk together in Christian love, striving for the advancement of God's kingdom in justice, righteousness, and mercy. We determine to promote the spirituality and prosperity of Christ's church by upholding his ordinances, practicing discipline, and following biblical teachings. Through the resources entrusted to us—spiritual gifts, time, and finances—we will contribute to the support of the ministry, the expenses of the church, the relief of the poor and oppressed, and to missions, home and abroad.

We also determine to foster spirituality in our families and in our own individual lives, to educate our children in the faith, and to seek to be the presence of Christ to our family and acquaintances. We resolve to walk carefully and responsibly in the world, to be salt and light in society, to be just in all our relationships and exemplary in lifestyle.

We further determine to care for one another in Christian love and concern, to uphold each other in prayer, to encourage each other, to help each other in all areas of life, and to be slow to take offense, but always ready for reconciliation, being mindful of the teaching and example of our Savior, Jesus Christ.

We moreover determine that when we move to a different location, we will unite with another congregation in order to continue to carry out the spirit of this covenant and the principles of God's Word.

E. *DENOMINATIONAL AFFILIATION*

It is the desire of this church to affiliate with and to cooperate with the _____ Baptist Association of the _____ Baptist Conference.

F. MEMBERSHIP

Any person professing faith in the Lord Jesus Christ as personal Savior, being baptized by immersion, adopting the views of faith and practice taught in the Bible and held by this church, may be admitted to membership. (For a detailed report on procedures and duties, please see the Bylaws, Section A.)

G. MEETINGS

This organization shall meet regularly for worship, study, fellowship, and business purposes as outlined in the Bylaws, Section B.

H. OFFICERS

The officers of this church shall be the pastor(s), the church board, and committees as provided for in the Bylaws, Section C. Each of the officers shall be a member of this church and shall subscribe fully to the Statement of Faith and Church Covenant given above.

I. CHURCH PROPERTY

1. This church shall have the power to receive, either by gift or purchase, and to hold such real, personal, or mixed property as is authorized by the laws of the state of _____ and is deemed necessary to fulfill the purpose and to carry out the business of the church, and shall have the power to dispose of such property by mortgage, deed, or otherwise. All such property shall be held in the name of the church. The Church Board shall have the power to receive, purchase, acquire, sell, lease, convey, mortgage, deed, or otherwise transfer property of the church, but only after having been duly authorized by the church at a regularly called business meeting. All contracts, notes, mortgages, conveyances, assignments, leases, releases, and other documents and papers in behalf of the church shall be executed by the Church Board.

2. In case of a division of the church (from which we pray to be spared by God's mercy to preserve us) the property of the church shall belong to those who abide by this Constitution.

3. In case of dissolution of the church organization, the property shall be assigned to the _____ Baptist Association of the _____ Baptist Conference. The church shall be considered dissolved if so decided by the membership, or when the church has not held an annual business meeting for three years, or when fewer than six members remain.

J. CHURCH YEAR

The fiscal year of the church shall begin on the first day of January and end on the last day of December.

K. CHURCH GOVERNMENT

The church body, at its annual, quarterly, and special business meetings, is the legislative and governing body of this organization.

L. REVISION OF THE CONSTITUTION

1. The church body may make changes or additions to the Constitution at any quarterly or special business meeting. The changes or additions shall be submitted to the members in writing (hand delivered or mailed to the last known address) at least four months prior to such a meeting. Preliminary approval must be give at a quarterly or special business meeting at least three months prior to final adoption.

2. Changes or additions must be approved by a three-quarter majority of the votes cast.

3. Sections B, C, and L3 are irrevocable and unalterable.

BYLAWS

A. MEMBERSHIP

1. Admission

(a) *Procedure*: All persons seeking membership in this church shall appear before the Church Board to be examined. Upon approval by the Board such persons shall be recommended to the church body and shall give testimony of their faith to the church body at any business session. A time for questions will be allowed and a vote will be taken. Upon acceptance, the hand of fellowship shall be extended to the person seeking membership at a Communion service.

(b) *Requirements*: Personal profession of faith publicly expressed in baptism followed by growth toward a Christlike lifestyle.

2. Transfer

Letters of transfer, for the purpose of uniting with another church, shall be granted by the church body upon recommendation by the Church Board.

3. Discipline

It shall be the duty of the Edification Coordinator, working with appropriate committees, to seek to reclaim those members who disregard their Covenant obligations; this shall be done in keeping with Matthew 18:15-17 and Galatians 6:1-2. If said member cannot be reclaimed, the

Coordinator shall present to the Board and subsequently to the church body a recommendation that the said member shall no longer be a member of this church. Upon approval of said recommendation, that member's name shall be deleted from the membership list and he/she shall be notified whenever possible.

4. *Restoration*

Any person whose name was deleted from the membership list, requesting restoration of membership, shall appear before the Church Board to be examined. Reinstatement by vote of the church body may then follow.

5. *Withdrawal*

When a member requests that his/her name be deleted from the membership, the Edification Coordinator shall interview the person and give counsel if desired. When satisfied that such member wishes to pursue the request, the Coordinator shall advise the Board and the church body of this request and the member's name shall be deleted from the list.

6. *Nonresidency*

Members, upon moving, are encouraged to furnish the Edification Coordinator with a mailing address; they are encouraged to begin at once to seek out and fellowship with another church of like faith and practice where possible.

B. *CHURCH MEETINGS*

1. *Devotional Meetings*

The church shall meet regularly each Sunday for worship, Bible study, and fellowship purposes. They shall observe the Lord's Supper every month or more frequently at the discretion of the Church Board. They shall meet at other times as the church may decide in keeping with the Church Covenant, as outlined in the Constitution.

2. *Business Meetings*

a) The annual business meeting shall be held no later than the fourth week of January for the purpose of recognizing those involved in the growth and life of the church; for receiving the budget, annual reports, projected goals and planning of Committees; for transacting of appropriate business and concluding with a challenge for the coming year.

b) In addition to the regular quarterly business meetings, special business meetings may be called at any time by the Pastor, or the Church Board or by the Clerk upon written request by a quorum of the members of the church body. Notice of such meeting, and the object for which it is called, shall be read from the pulpit at least two Sundays in advance of the meeting.

c) Thirty percent of the qualified members shall constitute a quorum except for the calling of a Pastor, when forty percent shall be required. The meeting shall be rescheduled if a quorum has not been reached within thirty minutes after the posted time.

d) The goal of the church body shall be unanimity in all decisions; however, a simple majority shall be sufficient to carry any motion except where otherwise provided in the Constitution or Bylaws.

C. *CHURCH OFFICERS*

1. *Pastor*

a) The Pastor must adhere to the basic doctrines of faith as outlined in the Church Covenant and Statement of Faith and to historic Baptist principles. The Pastor is subject to the qualifications of 1 Timothy 3:1-13.

b) When the pastorate is vacant or when adding another Pastor, a pulpit committee shall be formed, composed of three members from the Church Board and an equal number of members appointed by the church body. The calling of a Pastor shall come before the church body at any regular or specially called business meeting. A vote of three-fourths of those qualified members present and voting shall be required to extend a call. The Pastor shall be called for an indefinite period of time and at least one month's notice must be given by the Pastor or by the church for the termination of his or her ministry unless otherwise agreed to.

c) Job Description (omitted)

2. *Church Board*

a) Members of the Church Board shall be persons of irreproachable Christian character, having a "good report" (1 Timothy 3:1-13).

b) A Church Board of six members (including Pastor and Moderator) for the first one hundred members or portion thereof and one additional member for each fifty members or portion thereof above one hundred is recommended, but not mandatory. Approximately one-third of the Board membership (excluding Pastor) shall be elected at each annual election for a term of three years.

c) This annual election shall be held during the first full week of December, but may be rescheduled when necessary by the Church Board. Nominees for election shall be presented to the church at least two full weeks prior to the election. If nominations are made from the floor, such nominees are to have given prior consent. Elected members shall assume office January 1, following their election. Termination of said office shall be by written letter and is effective when stated. The Church Board has the authority to fill a vacant position until the coming election.

d) Job Description

i) The Church Board will be responsible to the church body for providing leadership for the ministries of the church.

ii) The Board will follow a specified schedule for regular monthly meetings as worked out in advance.

iii) One Church Board member will be elected to act as coordinator for each of the major church ministries—worship, edification, outreach, resources. To assist in this task, standing committees may be formed as outlined in paragraph 4 below. The coordinator will chair the respective standing committee. Other Board members may serve on these committees as needed. All such appointments are subject to congregational approval.

iv) The Board will approve disbursement of the Benevolent Fund.

3. *Moderator*

a) The Moderator shall be elected by the church membership for a three-year term, which is coterminous with and constitutes election to the Church Board.

b) As a Church Board member, the moderator is subject to the appropriate qualifications.

c) The Moderator shall chair church business meetings and Church Board meetings or appoint another Board member in the case of the Moderator's absence.

d) Business sessions shall follow parliamentary procedure as set forth in *Robert's Rules of Order*.

4. *Standing Committees*

a) To assist the Church Board in the fulfillment of its tasks, standing committees may be formed, each of which should carry one major area of responsibility (i.e., worship, edification, outreach, resources).

b) Members of standing committees, as helpers, shall be worthy of respect, etc. (1 Timothy 3:9-13).

c) Committee members shall be nominated by the committee chairperson, approved by the Church Board, and voted on by the congregation.

d) Duties of standing committees (or the respective coordinator in the absence of an established committee) are as follows:

   i) Worship: to coordinate the efforts of the congregation in fulfilling its worship mandate.

     —evaluating the worship life of the congregation.

     —educating the congregation in worship life.

     —administrating worship-related church ministries, e.g., music program.

  ii) Edification: to coordinate the efforts of the congregation in fulfilling its edification mandate.

     —evaluating the edification life of the congregation.

     —administrating education-related church ministries, e.g., Sunday school, children's clubs, youth.

     —fostering inter-church fellowship which provides for the nurturing of the membership.

     —seeking to meet cases of special need, whether financial, spiritual, etc.

 iii) Outreach: to coordinate the efforts of the congregation in fulfilling its outreach mandate.

     —evaluating the outreach of the congregation.

     —administrating outreach-related church ministries, including evangelism, discipleship, missions, and social action projects.

 iv) Resources: to coordinate the efforts of the congregation in providing material resources for the purpose of fulfilling its mandate.

     —To this end, the committee shall be divided into three subcommittees.

    (1) The Finance Committee to oversee the receiving and disbursing of all funds. After evaluating current needs and past giving trends, they shall arrive at a budget for the coming year; this is to be presented to the Board for consideration by the first Sunday in January, and to the church body for approval at the yearly business meeting.

    (2) The Facilities Committee to arrange for the needed building space and equipment, ushering services, etc., to insure smooth operation during times of meeting. Purchase of or selling of land and buildings shall be recommended to the Board, and after careful deliberation, recommendation shall be made to the church body for approval.

    (3) Publicity Committee to coordinate advertising as prearranged by each committee or as directed by the Board.

     —The Coordinator of Resources shall nominate for Board and

church approval for a term of one year, a Church Clerk and assistant to record the business meetings, write official church letters, keep an active filing system, report to the denominational publication, Association, Conference, etc.

—The Coordinator of Resources shall nominate for Board and church approval for the term of one year a qualified treasurer, financial secretary, auditors, etc., as needed to handle the financial matters of the church.

—The Coordinator of Resources shall ensure that a Nominating Committee is appointed: three from the Board, three from the church at large, the Pastor, and this coordinator as ex-officio members. This Committee shall be appointed by the church body at the annual business meeting and shall prepare the ballot for the coming year's election.

D. *REPRESENTATION AT THE ASSOCIATION AND CONFERENCE*

Each year, delegates shall be appointed by the congregation to represent the church at the Association and/or Triennial Conference. The duties of these delegates shall be to furnish to the Association and/or Conference a statement of the conditions of the church in a manner prescribed; to represent faithfully the desires of the church; to cooperate with the delegates of other churches in advancing the kingdom of God; and to report back to the church on matters of importance.

E. *AMENDMENTS OF BYLAWS*

These Bylaws may be altered or amended by a two-thirds vote of the voting members present at any regular business meeting of the church. The proposed changes shall have been presented in written form to each member at least two weeks prior to such meeting.

Organizational Structure of the Local Church

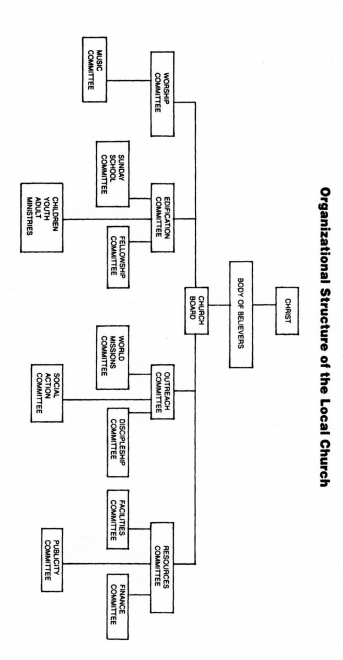

2 Selected Dates in Baptist History

1609	Formation of a Baptist church in Amsterdam under John Smythe
1639	Formation of a Baptist church in Providence, Rhode Island, under Roger Williams
1641	First Particular Baptist Church formed in England
1670	Association of Rhode Island churches organized
1671	Seventh Day Baptist congregation formed in Newport, Rhode Island
1707	Philadelphia Association organized
1763	Founding of Baptist Church in Horton, Nova Scotia, Canada
1775	Black church present among slaves in Silver Bluff, South Carolina
1801	Seventh Day Baptist General Conference formed
1814	Triennial Convention formed
1824	Founding of the American Baptist Publication Society
1832	Founding of the American Baptist Home Mission Society
1843	German Baptist church founded in Philadelphia
1845	Organization of the Southern Baptist Convention
1852	Swedish Baptist Church formed in Rock Island, Illinois
1870	Formation of the General Association of General Baptists

1880   Organization of the Baptist Union of Ontario and Quebec

1895   Organization of the National Baptist Convention

1905   Founding of the Baptist World Alliance
        Organization of the American Baptist Association (Landmark)

1906   Convention of Atlantic Baptists (Canada) established

1907   Establishment of the Northern Baptist Convention

1909   Establishment of the Baptist Union of Western Canada

1915   National Baptist Convention separates into incorporated and unincorporated denominations

1932   General Association of Regular Baptists formed

1943   Formation of the Conservative Baptist Foreign Mission Society

1944   Formation of the Baptist Federation of Canada

1946   Formation of the Baptist Joint Committee on Public Affairs

1947   Organization of the Conservative Baptist Association of America

1950   Northern Baptist Convention name changed to the American Baptist Convention

1953   Formation of the Fellowship of Evangelical Baptist Churches in Canada

1961   Progressive National Baptist Convention formed

1970   Union of French Baptist Churches of Canada joins Baptist Federation of Canada

1972   American Baptist Convention name changed to American Baptist Churches in the U.S.A.

3 ❀ Resources for Further Study

I. General Information

Jacquet, Constant H., Jr., ed., *Yearbook of American and Canadian Churches 1983*. Nashville: Abingdon Press, 1983.

Mead, Frank S., *Handbook of Denominations in the United States*. Seventh Edition. Nashville: Abingdon Press, 1980.

Melton, John Gordon, *The Encyclopedia of American Religions*. Wilmington, N.C.: McGrath Publishing Company, 1978.

Piepkorn, Arthur C., *Profiles in Belief: The Religious Bodies of the United States and Canada*, Vol. 2: *Protestantism*. New York: Harper & Row, Publishers, 1978.

II. Baptist History

Armstrong, O. K. and Marjorie, *The Indomitable Baptists*. New York: Doubleday, 1967.

Estep, William R., *The Anabaptist Story*. Grand Rapids: Wm. B. Eerdmans Pub. Co., 1975.

Lord, Fred Townley, *The Baptist World Fellowship*. London: The Carey Kingsgate Press, 1955.

Shaw, Bynum, *Divided We Stand: The Baptists in American Life*. Durham, N.C.: Moore Publishing Co., 1974.

Torbet, Robert G., *A History of the Baptists*. Rev. ed. Valley Forge: Judson Press, 1973.

III. Baptist Doctrine

Cook, Henry, *What Baptists Stand For*. London: The Carey Kingsgate Press, 1947.

Hudson, Winthrop S., *Baptist Convictions*. Valley Forge: Judson Press, 1959.

Mullins, E. Y., *Baptist Beliefs*. Valley Forge: Judson Press, 1925.

Wallace, Oates Charles S., *What Baptists Believe*. Nashville: Sunday School Board, 1934.

IV. Baptist Polity

Hiscox, Edward T., *The Hiscox Standard Baptist Manual*. Valley Forge: Judson Press, 1965 (based on *The New Directory for Baptist Churches*, 1894).

Maring, Norman H. and Hudson, Winthrop S., *A Baptist Manual of Polity and Practice*. Valley Forge: Judson Press, 1963.

McNutt, William Roy, *Polity and Practice in Baptist Churches*. Valley Forge: Judson Press, 1935.

Sullivan, James L., *Baptist Polity As I See It*. Nashville: Broadman Press, 1983.

4 Questions for Reflection and Interaction

Chapter 1

1. What relationship ought to exist between God's nature and that of the church? In what ways can your congregation be a mirror of God's own nature?
2. How ought the concept of God's kingdom affect the goals and practices of your congregation?
3. Does your church look primarily forward or backward?
4. Why is it important for a congregation to have a clear understanding of the nature and purpose of the church?
5. Does your congregation have a covenant or a statement of faith?

Chapter 2

1. What are the advantages and disadvantages of denominational affiliation? Of ecumenical affiliation?
2. How is the concept of covenant implemented in your congregation?
3. In what ways are the three aspects of Christ's mandate to the church being followed in your congregation?
4. To what extent is the glorification of God the central aim of the activities of your congregation?

Chapter 3

1. What role do you see given to the Holy Spirit in the observances of the ordinances in your congregation?
2. Ought there be a place for the use of the ordinances in the evangelistic activity of the church?
3. Does your congregation tend to emphasize the ordinance aspect or the sacrament aspect of the sacred observances?
4. In what sense can participation in the ordinances be seen as anticipatory "pre-enactment" of the future kingdom of God?

Chapter 4

1. Which of the three New Testament emphases concerning baptism is stressed in your congregation?
2. What is the position of your congregation concerning persons baptized by some other mode, but desiring to join your fellowship?
3. What role does baptism play in the process of salvation?
4. Do you understand your baptism more as personal testimony, gospel proclamation, or God's act of regeneration?
5. How might a congregation make a baptismal service a festive celebration?

Chapter 5

1. In what sense are the five basic themes concerning the Lord's Supper interdependent?
2. What might cause a believer to refrain from participating in the Lord's Supper?
3. The Lord's Supper is generally a solemn occasion. Why? In what way could the joyfulness of the event be expressed?
4. Is it proper to celebrate the Lord's Supper at retreats, camps, conferences, etc?
5. Does your congregation stress "Eucharist," "Communion," or "Lord's Supper" in its celebrations? How?

Chapter 6

1. What are the implications of viewing church membership as a covenant?
2. Is local church membership necessary? What are its advantages and disadvantages?
3. Is church membership too formalized today?
4. Does your congregation effectively integrate church discipline with church membership?
5. What does church membership mean to you?

Chapter 7

1. Does your congregation emphasize its associational or denominational ties? If not, why not? If so, how?
2. What form of church government does your congregation practice? How is this evidenced?
3. What decisions would a church board that follows democratic congregationalism make without consulting the congregation as a whole?
4. How is the priesthood of all believers demonstrated in the life of your congregation?

Chapter 8

1. Compare and contrast your congregation's structure with the proposal in the book.
2. What would be the strengths and weaknesses of the proposal if it were implemented in your situation?
3. Should pastors be called to a congregation on some contract basis?
4. In what ways do your congregation's leaders practice servant leadership?

Chapter 9

1. If you were a delegate to an ordination council, what questions would be uppermost in your mind?
2. In addition to local pastors, what other Christian workers ought to be ordained?
3. What would be the proper response of a congregation which has been advised by an associational council not to proceed with the ordination of one of its members?
4. What positions in your congregation and denomination are currently open for women? What is your opinion concerning women in ministry?

Chapter 10

1. What was the role of the Bible in Baptist beginnings?
2. What similarities and differences do you see in the three separate beginning points discussed in the chapter?
3. How has the transition from dissenting minority to acceptance by the religious establishment affected Baptists in America?
4. To what extent does your congregation emphasize its Baptist heritage?

Chapter 11

1. What is the relationship between the authority of Scripture and the contributions of tradition, reason, and experience in your life? In the life of your congregation?

2. How does "individual competency" come to expression in your congregation?
3. What are the implications of the Baptist heritage for contemporary church-state issues? Which current issues are most significant?
4. To what extent are the seven convictions discussed in the chapter relevant for the contemporary situation?

Chapter 12

1. Has the BWA been an asset or a hindrance to the work of God in the world?
2. What are the advantages and disadvantages of congregational support for cooperative organizations, such as those mentioned in this chapter?
3. Should the church seek to influence governmental decisions? If not, why not? If so, in what ways?
4. Why have Baptists experienced such phenomenal growth in the United States in comparison to other countries?

Chapter 13

1. What are the advantages and disadvantages of the presence of so many independent Baptist fellowships?
2. What is the role of your congregation in, and its responsibility to, the fellowship of which it is a part? What is your denomination's responsibility to your congregation?
3. Compare the advantages and disadvantages of fellowships which are homogeneous (based on doctrinal, ethnic, or regional homogeneity) with those which are more pluralistic?
4. What is your evaluation of the future of the Baptist movement?